THE
VICTORIAN
KITCHEN

The Victorian Kitchen was originally published to enhance the major BBC television series of the same name.

Jennifer Davies was Associate Producer of *The Victorian Kitchen Garden*, *The Victorian Kitchen* and *The Victorian Flower Garden*, all shown on BBC Television. She was born and brought up in rural Herefordshire where, when not involved in making programmes, she continues to run her own smallholding.

Also published by BBC Books

The Victorian Kitchen Garden
The Victorian Kitchen Garden Companion
Ruth Mott's Favourite Recipes
The Victorian Flower Garden

The Victorian Kitchen

JENNIFER DAVIES

BBC BOOKS

I wish to express my grateful thanks to each person who took the time and trouble to talk to me about their memories of how kitchens used to be. I am equally indebted to those kind persons who loaned reference books and archive photographs. Thank you also to the librarians of The Fuller Collection at Oxford Polytechnic, The Museum of English Rural Life, Reading and the BBC Reference Library, Bristol. For their editorial guidance and unstinting help I thank Heather Holden-Brown and Sarah Hoggett and, for the care that she has taken with the design of this book, Linda Blakemore. Thanks must also go to Robert Hill for his photographs.

I would also like to take this opportunity to express gratitude to Colonel and Mrs John Ward and Captain Gerald Ward for their continued kind assistance and interest.

There wouldn't have been a book without a television series and there wouldn't have been a series without the skill and dedication of my colleagues. I particularly thank the producer, Keith Sheather, who, by taking the brunt of programme-making, allowed me to write this book.

Last, but by no means least, I thank the presenter, Peter Thoday and, because they *were* the series, Ruth Mott, Alison Arnison and Harry Dodson.

Published by BBC Books
a division of BBC Enterprises Ltd
Woodlands, 80 Wood Lane, London W12 0TT

First published in hardback 1989
Reprinted 1989 (three times)
Reprinted 1990
First published in paperback 1991

© Jennifer Davies 1989

ISBN 0 563 36281 2

Typeset in 11/13pt Monophoto Garamond
and printed and bound in Great Britain by
Butler & Tanner Ltd, Frome
Colour separations by Technik, Berkhamsted
Colour printing by Lawrence Allen
Jacket printed by Belmont Press Ltd, Northampton
Cover printed by Clays Ltd, St Ives plc

CONTENTS

·

INTRODUCTION *Page 7*

CHAPTER ONE · The Lay-out *Page 11*

CHAPTER TWO · The Mistress of the House *Page 19*

CHAPTER THREE · The Servants of the House *Page 27*

CHAPTER FOUR · Kitchen Fittings *Page 51*

CHAPTER FIVE · Victorian Values *Page 69*

CHAPTER SIX · The Kitchen and the Garden *Page 81*

CHAPTER SEVEN · Preserving *Page 93*

CHAPTER EIGHT · Shopping *Page 103*

CHAPTER NINE · Breakfast *Page 115*

CHAPTER TEN · Luncheon *Page 125*

CHAPTER ELEVEN · Tea *Page 133*

CHAPTER TWELVE · Dinner *Page 139*

CHAPTER THIRTEEN · Supper *Page 147*

CHAPTER FOURTEEN · Beverages *Page 153*

CHAPTER FIFTEEN · Charity *Page 157*

CHAPTER SIXTEEN · Alexis Soyer *Page 159*

Victorian Recipes *Page 165*

Bibliography *Page 185*

Index *Page 187*

INTRODUCTION

.

Harry Dodson

'The farmer wants a wife, the farmer wants a wife...' and in the same vein as that old nursery rhyme, the Victorian Kitchen Garden wanted a kitchen. So we gave it one.

It had all begun in 1984. That was when retired head gardener Harry Dodson, helped by a television production team (including myself) and a horticultural historian called Peter Thoday, had decided to turn the gardening clock back a hundred years.

One of the high-walled old kitchen gardens on the country estate where Harry lives was cleaned up, the weeds vanquished and the glasshouses restored.

The object of the exercise was two-fold. The extraordinary wealth of different varieties once found in nineteenth-century kitchen gardens had, over the years, become decimated by fashion and EEC regulations. These old vegetables and fruits had a diversity of shape and flavour which provided beauty in the garden and variety in the kitchen. We wanted to recapture both. The second objective was to try and record, before it was too late, the skills a Victorian gardener needed. For despite the vagaries of the seasons and lack of modern chemicals and devices, he had to supply the master and his family, the guests and all the servants, with quality and quantity of produce every day of the year. That's where we were lucky with Harry Dodson. He had learned his skills from men who in turn had learned their know-how from Victorian gardeners. Harry still used many of the old techniques. Our Victorian kitchen garden, complete with its nineteenth-century varieties, was a success and grew productive and beautiful.

That's when the murmur went round ... the garden needs a kitchen. In such a place the garden produce could once again provide a fitting accompaniment to a whole range of dishes. Here too, recipes of the period could be tried using authentic Victorian methods and utensils. The recreation of the walled kitchen garden had revealed the delights and drudgeries of an enclosed, almost forgotten, institution. Could we do the same for its companion, the kitchen?

It had been difficult (before I discovered Harry Dodson) to find a Victorian kitchen garden to restore. It was even more difficult to find a Victorian kitchen. Clean white cookers, microwaves and mixers on wipe-down units and someone who pops in to help so many hours a week, are what is 'below stairs' today. But I had a stroke of luck, or at least a lucky recall of memory. At the time that I was looking for old gardening relics I had been advised to go and see a fine example of glass coping on a wall in a kitchen garden some dozen miles from our Victorian kitchen garden. The return journey from that garden necessitated walking through a cobbled courtyard with buildings on either side, the house itself being some distance away. The right-hand buildings had been converted into sensible, smart storage places; the left-hand buildings had not. A passing glance at one of the cobwebbed windows registered a rusty iron range inside. This chance sighting was forgotten until the Victorian kitchen idea got under way. In the meantime, the mansion had changed hands. It was more than likely that the buildings had now been renovated and the range removed and anyway, would the new owners welcome interest from a television company? It was a slender chance. We were lucky on both scores: the buildings had not been renovated and we were allowed to go and look at them. To our delight we saw beneath crumbling ceilings a store cupboard with wooden shelving, a larder with slate slabs and iron hooks, and around the corner from this another larder with white tiled walls and a gauze wire window. From the larders a cobwebby passageway led into a 20-foot-long scullery. Dense laurel bushes outside the windows made the light in the scullery shadowy, but it was sufficient to reveal two large sinks, one wooden and one glazed. Beside these, still upright but frail and rotten, stood a tall wooden plate rack. To the right of the plate rack was a half-open door through which we could see the kitchen proper – a barn of a room, with a ceiling which soared to 20 feet.

The kitchen range was set into the wall opposite the scullery door, cupboards were against one wall and shelving with cupboards beneath against another. One wall was completely bare. In the centre of the kitchen, where once the kitchen table would have stood, was a varied assortment of bedroom furniture. This kitchen with its larders had been locked up by the wife of the previous owner four decades ago. It wasn't that she didn't like the kitchen, it was that she didn't like the shape of the mansion. Builders were instructed to remove a great chunk from the middle of the house. This left the right-hand side standing on its own as the 'new' mansion and the left-hand side containing the kitchen complex, some distance away, locked and forgotten. That was how we found the kitchen.

Finding the Victorian cook to go in it was, as people say, another story. If Harry Dodson had learned traditional gardening methods in old estate gardens by serving his apprenticeship under old-style head gardeners, then it was likely that somewhere were women who had served their apprenticeship in mansion kitchens under old-style cooks. To put this theory to the test, we wrote to various journals about the Victorian kitchen idea, and our need for practical information and reminiscences.

We were lucky in that at this time *The Victorian Kitchen Garden* series was being shown on television every week so at least people knew us. It wasn't long before the contents of the office postbag had to be divided into two piles: letters about the garden and letters from ladies who had, half a century and more ago, been kitchenmaids.

The letters made extraordinary reading. Our hopes were confirmed. Just as Victorian methods and regimes had endured in the mansion garden through to the first quarter of this century, so had they too in the kitchen. It gave me tremendous pleasure to meet some of the letter writers, so clear was their recall and so absorbing their anecdotes. I am indebted to ladies too numerous to mention personally but who contributed facts and stories which brought alive, as no history book could, working days in kitchens which still employed Victorian methods and principles.

Ruth Mott was one of the women who wrote to us after reading our article in the Women's Institute journal *Home and Country*. Standing in the kitchen of her cottage near Newbury in Berkshire, she thought back to the days when, in 1930, she had been a scullery maid in a big country house. She sat down to describe some of the jobs she had had to do. The following is a little of what she wrote:

Ruth Mott

Washing up in a teak sink with only soda and soft soap to help, hands red raw from dashing over to the large vegetable sink, so deep I had a little box to stand on!

The vegetable gardener called in at 7.30 am to pick up the order for the day, returning with a wheelbarrow full of veg. at about 9. With 18 staff a lot of food was required. Savoys and swedes so frozen they had to be chopped – seakale, salsify and scorzonera, seldom heard of now. Grating horseradish, tears streaming down the face.

Birds to pick, hares and rabbits to skin. Old-fashioned ice boxes with basins underneath, ice caves to pack for iced soufflés. Hampers to pack for shooting lunches ... Christmas puddings made in the middle of the scrubbed table, yes and lambtails to be skinned for pies. Roasting on a spit and Dutch ovens.

Sauces and soups rubbed through tammy cloths.

Five wheelbarrows of coal being tipped under the stove to keep the fire going for the day ...

I've worked long hours, hard, had many laughs and met some lovely people ...

I don't know whether the *Victorian Kitchen* production team could be described as lovely people but Ruth soon met us too. She also ended up, I'm afraid, working long hours again, for one thing led to another and, to our delight, she became the Victorian cook.

Under the watchful eye of our designer, Sally Hulke, the kitchen and larders were restored as much as possible. Dead birds and twigs were removed from the range chimney. On the range itself, broken iron encasing the back flue had to be welded and the whole range sanded inside and out to get rid of the rust. Despite all our efforts, the right-hand oven obstinately refused to climb to anything near the temperature in the left-hand oven:

it was something we would have to live with. A defect in one of the flues also meant that on foggy, windless days, smoke went not up the chimney, but oozed copiously out of every crack in the range that it could find and filled the kitchen. This added authenticity to our project but occasioned the frequent mass exodus of the film crew. It quickly became apparent, too, how soon coal fumes could tarnish the copper utensils that now furnished the kitchen.

It was something of a minor miracle that these copper pots, pans and moulds furnished the kitchen at all. Such specimens, once the apple of every cook's eye, can still be found in specialist antique shops, but their price tags equal their handsome appearance. Large mansion kitchens needed a lot of 'coppers' but, rather depressingly, our programme budget was just not up to buying them. Fate lent a kindly hand in the form of the owners of two large houses in different parts of the country. Although their house kitchens had long been modernised, many of the old kitchen fittings and fixtures were still kept in the basement and we were able to borrow them. This was a double blessing, for amongst the collections were articles which it would have been almost impossible to buy – for example, a wooden and zinc refrigerator, a waist-high pestle and mortar made from a tree trunk, and a metal ice-cream mould in the shape of a monstrous strawberry. With the help of Dorothy Elliott, our enthusiastic and expert properties buyer, articles for the scullery and larder were easier to find. Dorothy combed antique markets until she came across the appropriate articles.

Unable to provide Ruth with a complete complement of scullery maid, second kitchenmaid and first kitchenmaid, not to mention an odd-job man and a vegetable girl, we found Alison Arnison for her. Alison was a recently married young music teacher who worked from home. She was slender, blonde and ethereal-looking, with long musician's fingers. When one considers the inordinately heavy copper saucepans, the smutty coal scuttle and the complete absence of helpful culinary gadgets in our Victorian kitchen, one must also add, that Alison was brave too.

With Alison to help Ruth demonstrate old culinary methods, Harry Dodson to supply the garden produce and presenter Peter Thoday filling in the historical background, we recorded the television series *The Victorian Kitchen*. Because of time strictures and because somehow there are some things which just can't be translated into television pictures, there were facts about Victorian kitchens which inevitably couldn't be fitted in to the series. I hope that this book fills those gaps and that you enjoy it.

Jennifer Davies

Alison Arnison

CHAPTER ONE

The Lay-out

If a cook is half suffocated she cannot possibly do her work properly; and her stomach will be so upset, to say nothing of her temper, that she will be incapable of tasting and seasoning her dishes to suit the palates of her employers.

A dire mid-nineteenth-century warning indeed! But what could the concerned Victorian householder do to prevent his palate being inconvenienced in this way? One solution, for people who had money, was to make sure his kitchen was large and lofty.

Their loftiness (especially if a ventilation hole was set high enough into the wall) also encouraged kitchen smells to drift away from the main part of the house. Culinary odours were an embarrassment to the Victorian houseowner. If the residence was small, the kitchen was generally in the basement and connected with the family rooms by a door at the top of a flight of stairs. Covering this door with heavy green baize went some way towards stopping kitchen smells seeping through and giving guests an

A cook at her board with kitchenmaids in attendance. The open doorway leads to the scullery

unwelcome olfactory preview of their dinner. In addition certain 'anti-smell' rules were adhered to in the kitchen itself. Grease must not be allowed to fall and burn in the oven and, at the slightest hint that it had, the oven was fumigated by burning hay or straw inside it. A crust of bread was always put into water in which green vegetables were boiled and, after cooking, the greens water was taken outside and poured away in a corner of the garden. If there was no garden, it could be poured down the sink but had to be followed by carbolic acid.

On the same principle that the 'kitchen and scullery should never assert their nearness through the nose', houseowners went to great lengths, quite literally, to distance the dining room from the kitchen. In large houses, a serving hatch connected the kitchen to a passageway. The hatch was kept tightly shut except when dishes had to be passed through. The passageway, which might as an extra precaution have a door in it, led by a long and circuitous route to the dining room. No staircase led off the passage for fear that smells would travel up the stairs; and every so often ducts were placed in the passage wall to bring in fresh air from outside. These air ducts were particularly hazardous to serving maids or footmen trying to transport a soufflé and arrive in the dining room with it still risen. Such a sensitive dish often necessitated the bearer walking backwards in an attempt to block oncoming draughts.

If the kitchen was in the basement, food travelled up to a serving room (a room with a plain dresser in it, next to the dining room) by means of a lift. The servants themselves went up a flight of steps called the dinner stairs, which came out next to the butler's pantry.

Above: Dish cover

As the original lay-out of most big Victorian houses remained unchanged until well into this century, the task of keeping food hot between kitchen and plate was one which occupied several generations of kitchen staff. To ensure that food was still hot when it eventually arrived in the dining room, it had to leave the kitchen piping hot. Serving dishes covered by huge metal covers were heated well beforehand. Mistresses

Below: Hot water dish for entrées (left), dish for handing vegetables, dish for breakfast savouries

were known to run their finger lightly around their plates to check that they'd been heated properly. On the subject of heat, Mrs Gladys Fox of Downham Market told me that her employer had been so particular about having her food served hot that in an effort to comply with this, she had inadvertently melted a silver entrée dish. Tempers, too, could get overheated. The mistress of another one-time kitchenmaid liked her bacon hot and crisp. Hot, crisp bacon would leave the kitchen but with the combination of distance and the lady's maid not being ready to receive it, it often went soft. Notes of complaint would come back from her ladyship and the cook would take umbrage and blame the footman.

Sunbeams rarely strayed into Victorian kitchens for, in an attempt to keep them cool, their windows faced north or east, never south or west. The lower parts of the walls were covered in glazed bricks or tiles and the floors, particularly in large kitchens, were of stone. Wooden duckboards were placed on the floor at spots where a lot of standing was likely to be done (often by the large wooden table in the centre of the kitchen), but their effectiveness was limited. Ruth recalls working with women who, she says, had dreadful legs and feet as a result of standing for long hours on cold, stone floors.

Dressers gave shelf space for jugs, copper moulds and small utensils. Bigger utensils could be stored in the space beneath the dresser drawers. More shelves might be placed around the walls but a 'multiplicity of cupboards' about a kitchen was regarded as an evil because it encouraged untidiness and vermin. Pin-rails, on which metal dish covers could be hung, were positioned near the dresser. Also near the dresser was likely to have been a tall pestle and mortar. More often than not, the mortar was made out of part of a tree trunk with a marble basin inserted into the top. The pestle was a stout wooden pole with its bulbous base resting in the marble bowl and its top secured to the kitchen wall by a metal ring. The ring fitted sufficiently loosely to allow the pestle, when gripped with both hands, to be moved up and down in a pounding action. The huge pounder served many purposes, from breaking up ice or sugar to pounding meat down until it was fine enough to push through a sieve. We were lucky enough to borrow one of these huge pestle and mortars for our restored Victorian kitchen, but Ruth refused to go near it. She delegated all pounding jobs to Alison, saying that it was something she had never been able to master and had always hated. Any meat that she attempted to pound flew straight out of the bowl.

Looking like the other half of the tree trunk which made the mortar was usually a chopping block. This was always stood near the kitchen table. To the right or left of the kitchen fire, so that the contents would keep dry, was a large flour chest.

Apart from the serving hatch there were few openings to a kitchen. Doors encouraged visitors – unwelcome as the kitchen was a place of work. Two doors were generally the maximum. One might open to the outside and was a back route (often covered) into the house, and the other led directly into the room adjoining the kitchen, the scullery. Such an arrangement meant that to get from their quarters to the kitchen each morning, kitchen staff came down a back flight of stairs and into a passageway which led into the scullery. They would never go through the main house. There was an unwritten rule that no servant going to or from his or her quarters or working in the 'front' of the house was to be seen by the family or house guests. Where there was a staircase which unavoidably had to be used by both family and servants, the servants had to take especial care. It was not in the least unusual for a kitchenmaid to work for years for the same employer and never know what the front of his house looked like. ·

The scullery was just one of a number of rooms connected with the kitchen and the running of the house and was as dismal as its sounds. It had sinks, sometimes in the centre of the room but more often at the side beneath the windows for light. One sink might be made of wood and another of stone. The wooden one was less likely to chip any chinaware washed in it. All the kitchen pots, pans and servants' crockery were washed in the scullery. Near the sinks was a plate rack. It was attached to the wall or, if particularly large, stood on the floor. The scullery was also the place where the vegetables, fish and game were prepared. It contained a rough table as a useful work surface.

Many sculleries had boiling coppers. Some supplied hot water for the bedrooms and for cleaning. Others were used to boil kitchen cloths and, if the house was large, to boil vegetables. If the boilers were not stoked up the scullery would be cold and frequently wet as its floor was washed regularly. A drain in the corner took away water used to wash the floor.

The scullery might have a door to the outside yard but no direct door to any other room save the kitchen. A passageway acted as a buffer to stop steam from the scullery escaping into nearby store rooms.

The nearest store room to the scullery and kitchen was the pantry or dry larder. Here, bread, pastry, milk, butter and cold meats were kept. In large houses, the larders were often a series of outbuildings approached by a covered walkway leading off the back door of the scullery. These larders were whitewashed and had wire gauze instead of glass in the windows. The windows were placed opposite doorways so that there was a through draught. During very hot weather sheets of canvas were sometimes spread on the larder roofs and the surface constantly saturated with cold water.

The meat larder had hooks for hanging joints, a table and a chopping

Our larder, which at first sight needed more than disinfectant to put it right

block. The fish larder (or wet larder) had marble slabs with a feed of fresh water constantly running down them.

Both meat and fish larders had slate shelves and glazed tiles on the walls. The surfaces of both shelves and tiles had to be carefully wiped all over every morning and evening with flannel cloths wrung out in diluted disinfectant.

The vegetable store could be part of the meat or wet larder but, more often than not, it was a separate room conveniently close to both kitchen and scullery. In it vegetables were stored in square stone-sided compartments, one compartment to one type of vegetable. Bulkier produce like potatoes was put into larger enclosures at floor level.

Very grand houses could have as many as five larders, additional ones being for salting, smoking and storing bacon. In one of these Ruth had, in her early days, hand-cut every Monday morning sufficient rashers of bacon to last a staff of twenty-four for the whole week.

Dairies also formed part of the outbuildings or might be set out in the house grounds. The following is a most delightful description of a Victorian dairy as seen by a nineteenth-century writer:

It is situated at the back of the house, and sheltered by it from the mid-day and afternoon's sun, and from the morning's sun by a plantation, so that it is deliciously cool; it is about twelve feet long by ten wide, paved with flag stones, and the walls of plaster, like stone, a door at one end with a window above and a window high up at the other end, and two windows at the side; these have thin wire shutters and glazed sashes on hinges; the roof is of slate, with about two feet thickness of thatch over it; there are also several little openings for the admission of air, about one inch from the floor. A dressser, two feet wide, being two inches from the wall, is on both sides, and above these are two shelves of nine inches wide, also two inches from the wall supported on iron brackets. At the end, and opposite the door, is the churn, which is turned by a wheel outside, with apparatus for a donkey or mule to work it, if required. All the utensils are of sycamore wood and perfectly clean, never used twice without washing in hot water with soda put in, and made perfectly dry.

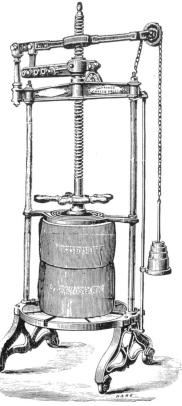

Nineteenth-century cheese press

For a Victorian client with £5000 to spend on a new house, an architect would design a mansion of about sixty rooms. Roughly half of these rooms would be used by the family and half as servants' working and living quarters. In a house of this size the cook and kitchenmaids could have the luxury of a pastry room. This room was a particular blessing in hot weather for, on a marble-topped table above deep drawers for storing flour and sugar, pastry could be made and stored well away from the heat of the kitchen range.

In the hinterland between the kitchen quarters and the 'front' of the mansion were rooms which, although connected to the kitchen, did not come under the cook's direct control. These rooms were the province of two other upper servants, the housekeeper and the butler.

The housekeeper (where there was no house steward at the head of the household) managed the smooth running of the house, although she did not dare interfere in the cook's domain. The housekeeper's personal room was part business and part parlour for, opposite her hearth and easy chair, deep high shelves and cupboards stretched from floor to ceiling. In these were stored preserves, pickles, spices, fancy groceries, cakes, sugar and biscuits. She was also responsible for looking after linen and the best china and leading off her room would be a small china closet complete with a sink and locking cupboards.

As the cook had her kitchenmaids, so the housekeeper had her own maids. Under her direction, they worked in a room called the still room. The room had a range and perhaps also a confectioner's oven. In the still room the housekeeper and her maids bottled fruit, made jam, crystallised fruits and flowers from the estate and baked cakes and biscuits. They also lightened the burden on the kitchen staff by making all the tea, coffee and soft drinks needed. Any wooden shelving put up in the still room was carefully painted so that the smell or 'flavour' of the wood would not permeate the articles placed on them.

STORE ROOM

An illustration from Anne Cobbett's book, The English Housekeeper *(1851)*

The housekeeper also kept a key to the store room. Here, within easy reach of the kitchen, were the bulk stores of goods such as flour, rice, tea and coffee. The latter two might be found in abundance if the family had connections with the British colonies. The store room was also a useful place for the economic practice of cutting up newly purchased soap. A piece of string was used to do this. The cut squares were then stacked so that air could circulate between them and make them harden and thus last longer. Candles also improved with keeping. 'March' candles were better than any other because, although they were made in the spring, they were not used until winter. Because of their smell, soap and candles were relegated to top shelves, well away from the other stored goods.

The housekeeper's world was far removed from that of the kitchen staff. When Ruth was a kitchenmaid, if she was halfway up a flight of stairs and the housekeeper appeared at the top, she knew that she must not pass her. Instead, she had to quickly scuttle right back to the bottom and, at a respectful distance, wait for the housekeeper to descend.

This lack of contact between the two became even more apparent on Mondays. On that day at 9 o'clock Ruth gave in her order for stocks from the store cupboard – soap, soda, flour, sultanas and so on. Later in the day, she went to collect the order – but not from the housekeeper's hands, instead her provisions were left outside the closed store-room door.

If the housekeeper was distant, then the butler was positively in another hemisphere for as Robert Kerr had said in his book *The Gentleman's House*, published in 1864: 'With the Kitchen the Butler may be said to have no intercourse whatever'. Kitchenmaids dealt instead with the footmen who worked under the butler, although they might see that great man and be favoured with a lofty 'good morning'.

The butler's domain was his pantry. In here were a pair of lead sinks with folding covers. In these sinks, all the tableware too valuable to be washed in the scullery was cleaned. Also, more curiously, was washed and dried any loose change the ladies of the house might have collected in their reticules. Here too, the butler might interview prospective hallboys and footmen, much as the cook recommended the hiring of kitchen and scullery maids.

If a house had valuable plate it was kept in a fire-proof safe in the butler's pantry. Even at night the butler could keep a watchful eye (or ear) on this safe for his bedroom generally led directly off the pantry. Last but not least, the butler also had responsibility for valuables of a more liquid kind. These lay in the wine and beer cellars which were also easily reached from the pantry.

CHAPTER TWO

The Mistress of the House

Your new home is not altogether in perpetual sunshine and the first shadow has fallen on it from the kitchen.

The mistresses of large houses were not the ones who worried about their cooks and kitchens. Wealthy enough to employ grand French chefs or experienced 'professed cooks' to take care of their culinary arrangements, and housekeepers to keep an eye on the lower servants, they were free to concentrate on silk dresses and setting a good example to inferiors. Their grindingly poor inferiors had no such troubles either – their concerns were more with eating at all. It was the middle classes who worried the merchants and industrialists, newly rich from being able to exploit natural resources by machinery, take advantage of spreading railways and use well-protected trade routes. When the middle-class husband went off to his office, his wife had to grapple with 'the servant difficulty'.

Victorian satirical journals were quick to exploit the mistress's difficulties

Cook. "WELL TO BE SURE, MUM! LAST PLACE I WERE IN, MISSIS ALWAYS KNOCKED AT THE DOOR AFORE SHE COME INTO *MY* KITCHEN!!"

Good cooks and kitchenmaids were scarce. Why? New-found wealth had wreaked several ironic twists of fate. Instead of sending their children to school the middle classes had them educated at home. This created a demand for intelligent girls who had received a smattering of accomplishments sufficient to enable them to become governesses. Without these refined accomplishments but with their innate intelligence, in former times these girls would have been loyal and able kitchenmaids and cooks – but alas no more. Yet the middle classes still needed servants in their newly built detached houses. Even though the calibre of servants was low, the demand for them was high.

In the last quarter of Victoria's reign, when it became more and more the fashion to have elaborate dinners, the worry of having inept kitchen staff intensified. The younger the mistress, the greater her problem. At home, before marriage, her mother had overseen all kitchen arrangements. She meanwhile had learned a little grammar, a little geography and filled the rest of her time with opera going and the latest fashions. With this background a young wife was ill-equipped to deal with the embarrassing problem of badly cooked and presented dishes spoiling her dinner parties.

From experience she knew how the dishes should taste, but she had no idea of how to make them taste so. She was in a quandary. It might be all right for German ladies to inhabit their kitchens, but English ladies were better employed directing and commanding from upstairs. She could learn to cook, but this would cause a social revolution – for if she blacked the grate, scrubbed the stairs and dished up the dinner, how could she at the same time be spotlessly, daintily and unflusteredly receiving callers? Also if wives became servants, forever in the kitchen, then they would be separated from their husbands and families who would remain in the drawing room. All this, not to mention the devastating effect servant-wives would have on fine table arrangements, was too terrible to contemplate.

Help was at hand – printed help, that is. For recognising the need, a plethora of well-intentioned advice was being written and published. A young wife was counselled to maintain a plan of action which would dispel her culinary worries. When invited out to dinner she was advised to monitor every dish brought to the table, taking a careful note of its appearance. This was in addition to having to listen and respond to her neighbour – but apparently abstracting her thoughts from conversation would become easier with practice. Looking at the food was not enough. She must also, despite the social convention that ladies should have slender appetites, taste every dish.

It was a good idea for the lady's maid to infiltrate the kitchen quarters of well-run houses. Whilst the lady was fulfilling her social obligations upstairs, the maid could take careful notes of how dishes were being made

Frontispiece of Consult me,
1883 edition

downstairs. 'Dressing' time could then be filled with the relaying of such information. This practice had the additional benefit of removing unsuitable gossip and ungracious silences from dressing time.

The reading of recipe books was also recommended. The French chef Ude (although old-fashioned, his book *The French Cook: or the art of cookery developed in all its branches* having been written in 1813) was considered good for 'scientific' cookery. More down to earth was Mrs Rundell's *A New System of Domestic Cookery* (1808). On the question of the exact amounts of ingredients, Dr William Kitchiner boasted in the third edition of his *The Cook's Oracle* (published in 1840) that his was the only English cookery book written from the real experience of a housekeeper and that his recipes were set down with a precision which had 'never before been attempted in Cookery books'. By 1845, Eliza Acton in *Modern Cookery for Private Families* was making recipes even more precise. She wrote the amount of ingredients needed clearly at the base of each recipe. However, the book which was probably the greatest help to the young middle-class wife was Isabella Beeton's *Book of Household Management*, published in 1861. Her recipes included the cost, cooking time and number of servings. Mrs Pender Cudlip (alias Annie Thomas) writing in the 1880s in *The Modern Housewife* says:

> I could not 'think out' a dinner my husband could eat without a cookery book, nor could I apportion out the righteous need of rations to each individual member of my household without having some indisputable precedent to go by, and this latter I found in Mrs Beeton's admirable 'Book of Household Management'.

The culinary knowledge gathered from reading and observing other people's dinner tables could be displayed by the young mistresses at precisely a quarter of an hour after breakfast every morning. This was the time when the cook came into the morning room or library or wherever the mistress happened to be, to discuss the meals for the day. Such meetings (if the cook was inexperienced) were also an opportunity to give a little lecture commenting on the proceedings of the previous day and 'advising on details' for the coming meals. In short, dazzled by the knowledge her mistress displayed, the cook would forget her own bad habits and adhere to her mistress's every word.

In fact, many mistresses who couldn't boil an egg were extraordinarily good at teaching their cooks. They knew exactly the correct food to have, the sauces which went with them and how everything should taste. It was only after the 1914–18 war and the subsequent shortage of servants that they foundered but here they were rescued, more often than not, by daughters who had had a few cooking lessons at school.

The teaching of cookery in schools stems back to a domestic economy

Left: Approving the daily menu

congress held at Manchester in 1878. The congress took place because a section of society was alarmed that English women were bad cooks and unable to manage their households properly. They wanted the old term of 'housewifery' turned into a new science called 'domestic economy', arguing that chemistry, science and natural philosophy had a bearing on what happened in the kitchen. One ambitious delegate, Sir Henry Cole, wanted a National College of Domestic Economy but this was thought to be a hammer to crack a nut and evidence of the 'tempest in a teapot' displayed by some at the congress. It was agreed that domestic economy should teach cooking, cleanliness, thrift, house rules for health, management of children and needlework.

In 1879 Leeds School Board began a course of instruction in practical cookery and cleaning for children in elementary schools. Girls were given printed recipes to take home and their parents were encouraged to buy cheaply, the food that their daughters prepared at school. By the 1890s, with formal education for girls gradually becoming more acceptable, domestic economy was being widely taught in girls' schools. Moveable gas stoves were wheeled into the classrooms and placed near an open grate for ventilation. In village schools where there was no gas, lessons took place around a kitchen range. As well as learning how to cook, the pupils were taught the mechanics of kitchen ranges, the chemistry of food and the importance of cleanliness – even down to how to press their fingernails into a bar of soap when no nailbrush was available.

A different sort of cookery school was Mrs A. B. Marshall's at 30 to 32 Mortimer Street, London. Mrs Marshall taught ladies the arts of superior cookery. By the late 1890s, her cookery book had sold 30 000

MARSHALL'S SCHOOL OF COOKERY,
30 & 32 MORTIMER STREET, REGENT ST., W.

Prospectus and Specimens of Daily Menus free on application or by post.

ALL THE TEACHING IS PERSONALLY CONDUCTED BY MRS. A. B. MARSHALL, AND IS ESSENTIALLY PRACTICAL.

Pupils are received by the day, course, or apprenticeship; resident or non-resident.

CERTIFICATES AND DIPLOMAS GRANTED.
For conditions see Prospectus.

Mrs Agnes Marshall

copies and the engravings in it of completed dishes are wonderful examples of artistic arrangement. Mrs Marshall was a shrewd businesswoman. At her premises she also had showrooms where every kitchen requisite could be purchased. She even sold ranges and gas cookers, her advertisements saying that she had practically tested and cooked with all the leading brands. A publication called *The World* reported the following:

On Entire Dinner Lesson Days the School of Cookery in Mortimer Street assumes the appearance of a culinary parliament. For seven consecutive hours Mrs. Marshall continues to arrest the attention of cooks and mistresses while she initiates them into the mysteries of dainty dishes.

In small houses where there was no grand morning room in which the cook could receive her instruction, each morning as soon after breakfast as possible, the mistress went to the kitchen. She looked in the larder to see what cold meat and pastry was still uneaten and based her meal orders on what she saw. She then went to the store cupboard, unlocked it and doled out any extra provisions the cook might need for the day. If items were required which weren't in either the larder or the store cupboard, she hurried out and bought them, making sure that she was back in time to receive morning visitors. Ever with an eye to economy, the mistress preferred to go herself rather than disrupt work in the kitchen by sending a maid.

In large houses, although there was little direct contact between the mistress and the lower kitchen staff her orders, whether given directly or via the cook, could still make the kitchenmaid's life a misery. Despite the fond Victorian belief that, 'except the relation of parent and child, nothing can be more beautiful than that sometime existing between the employer and employed' the relationship often got a little strained. Human memory, not books, records the discordant notes. One lady told me that many years ago her grandmother worked as a kitchenmaid and as she was preparing meat for the nursery her fingers inadvertently touched the meat. The mistress punished her by bringing a knife down onto her fingers.

Needless to say, the mistress's word was law no matter how far-fetched her whims might seem or how laborious for the staff. Another kitchenmaid was instructed to make a sponge cake for her mistress's dog. She did and used what remained of the mixture to make a cake for the servants' hall. Later in the week, the mistress enquired where the hall cake was. The girl told her she had made a sponge and that the servants had eaten it. The mistress was angry, saying that the servants' cake should always be a large fruit cake, to last, but without much fruit in it.

Demands for pets other than dogs could cause headaches in the kitchen. Potato peelings were boiled up to feed ducks and swans, this wasn't so bad but stale bread thrown by one master for amusement to the ducks on the lake continually encouraged rats into the kitchen. Some particularly irksome pet preparations might have to be carried out in the kitchen if the mistress kept birds. For instance she might take it into her head to feed them on 'German Paste'. For this, a small white loaf had to be soaked in water and the water then pressed out. The loaf was then put into an earthenware pan along with a 'nicely' grated carrot. Handfuls of barley-meal, from which the bran had been carefully sifted, were added and the whole lot mixed together with a pestle.

But the indignity of making bird paste in a busy kitchen was nothing to what the housemaid suffered if the mistress observed that her parrot was off colour and was pulling his feathers. The housemaid would have to effect a remedy by giving the parrot green capsicums and syringing him all over with salt and water for a few days.

From seeming to be annoyingly omnipresent, the mistress could be non-existent. This happened in large houses where there was a housekeeper and the kitchen staff might never see the mistress at all – except, that is, for her feet. Ruth recalls that this was all she ever saw of the mistresses of several of the houses she worked for, as they went by on the pavement above the kitchen window. Going to the other extreme kitchen staff did occasionally get spectacular glimpses. Apparently, especially if they had royalty to dinner, some ladies lingered obligingly outside their dressing-room before going down to dinner. Their kindly action was followed from below with eager eyes and indrawn breaths from maids brave enough to sneak upstairs and go the other side of the green baize door.

'If the mistress scolds, let the maid be mild, and above all, let her not scold again, or answer in an angry or insulting manner' – well-meaning advice, for if a maid couldn't bite her tongue she was liable to be given her marching orders on the spot. Servants could be instantly dismissed for what their employers considered to be disobedience, dishonesty or insobriety. They could even be dismissed too for no misdemeanour at all, provided that they were given a month's notice or wages in lieu.

But although the mistress's word was law, the person the kitchen staff most lived in fear and dread of was undoubtedly the cook.

CHAPTER THREE

The Servants of the House

I do not in the least admire gourmans, or gourmandism; and yet I would be more particular in selecting the servant who is to perform the business of preparing the food of the family, than I should deem it necessary to be in selecting any of the other servants.

 popular saying in Ruth's day was, 'Go to a good chef for presentation but go to a good cook for flavour'. Her Victorian counterparts had similar ideas on the subject.

Very grand houses had a French chef in the kitchen. In a circuitous way, many of these chefs were a by-product of the French Revolution. Having no aristocracy to employ them, many turned to restaurant work. They swelled the popularity of restaurants, making them increasingly places where the art of cooking was refined and elaborate. Aspiring young men trained in these restaurants and crossed the Channel to take up the post of chef in British households. For some, the journey ended in disappointment. Instead of being given the title 'Chef' they found that they were simply referred to as the 'French Cook'. The artistic dishes they

An employer's maxim: 'A girl should be encouraged to read in her leisure time, but it must be clearly understood that during working hours this is not to be attempted'

took such pains to prepare were often regarded as 'kickshaws' (over-elaborate dishes) by the master of the house who preferred a sirloin of beef or saddle of mutton. Sobriety, activity and zeal were not enough to make them popular; and even Queen Victoria is reputed to have eventually banished her chief chef Charles Francatelli, one-time pupil of the French master chef Carême, from the royal kitchens.

If chefs had a hard time with their employers they fared little better with their fellow servants who, having been instilled with an anti-French feeling from birth, regarded them with suspicion and distaste. (All, that is, except perhaps the under-housemaids, who according to a satirical writer of the time, were often captivated by the diamond shirt studs and varnished boots that French chefs wore when they sallied forth to the opera!) In all, it is hardly surprising that in the early part of Victoria's reign, before it became the fashion to dine late and have elaborate dishes, many chefs left private service, preferring to work in clubs and hotels.

'Professed cooks' were employed in big houses where no chef was kept. These women had worked their way up through the kitchen ranks, reaching the height of their profession. They were admired and feared and ruled their kitchens with a rod of iron. According to *The Servants' Practical Guide*, published in 1880, a professed cook was expected to do only the 'proper' cooking. The plain cooking and all the cleaning and scouring of the kitchen, scullery, larder, passages and kitchen utensils were done by the kitchen and scullery maids. This sort of cook had all her ingredients prepared for her and kitchenmaids to wait on her. The most junior member of the kitchen had to take a cup of tea up to her every morning before she got up to superintend the making of the dining-room breakfast at 5 minutes to 8. Being a senior servant, the cook had her own room but, like all the servants' rooms, it was on the top floor. Mrs Crosby from Stroud, now in her nineties, told me that as a scullery maid she had to climb 178 steps every morning up to a dome at the top of the house to deliver the cook's tea. All the servants' rooms led off the circle beneath the dome.

When the dining-room breakfast was over the cook wrote out onto a slate the day's luncheon and dinner menus. Some cooks also included the servants' hall meals. A footman or the cook herself would take the slate up to the mistress of the house for discussion.

In smaller houses, the mistress generally came down to the kitchen to see the cook. Before her visit the place was made spotless, a white cloth placed on the end of the table and the slate or a menu book and pencil placed on the cloth. Kitchenmaids were banished from the kitchen during the visit. One woman did tell me of an interesting exception to this ritual. Her mother had worked in a house where the mistress always insisted on

An illicit but successful combination of reading and working. The maid is near at hand to baste the meat in the hastener

seeing the cook in the evening to discuss the next day's menus. This meant that the cook, tired though she often was after preparing the evening meal, had to put on a clean white dress and apron and toil up the stairs at 10 o'clock every night.

The cook's morning work in the kitchen consisted of making pastries, jellies, creams or the more fancy dishes. After dishing-up the dining-room luncheon, she had the afternoon to herself – if there was no large dinner party to prepare for.

Her busiest time was 5 minutes to 9 in the evening when the dishing-up of dinner took place. This happened in a particularly tense atmosphere, the more so if there were a lot of guests in the dining room. Silence was maintained except for orders being given. In his *Manual of Domestic Economy* first published in 1857, J. H. Walsh captures the military regime needed to arrive successfully at this part of the day:

As Napoleon could always manage to assemble his troops on a given spot at a given time, from whatever distance they might have been drawn, so the cook, with a good head for her business, can contrive that all her dishes shall be ready.

When the clock struck, the dinner gong had to echo it. This required a combined effort from both the 'front' of the house and the kitchen. Ruth says she understood why some of the old cooks lost their tempers (and she knew all about cooks' tempers, because one had once stamped on a cake that she'd baked). If they were juggling with five or six courses and the meal time was suddenly brought forward or put back, fraught nerves were inevitable.

If dishes didn't appear on time, displeasure was made evident – albeit in a more restrained way – in the dining room. The master of the house would silently put his pocket watch onto the table, then look pointedly at the butler. The butler in turn looked at the footmen. The cook remained unaware of this, as no one dared go down to the kitchen.

In an attempt to avoid late meals and with the interesting observation that 'nothing can be done in perfection which be done in a hurry except catching Fleas', Dr William Kitchiner in *The Cook's Oracle* recommended that a clock in the dining room vibrate 'in unison' with a clock over the kitchen fire-place. Anne Cobbett, writing in *The English Housekeeper*, also recommended a clock but with the provision that:

... the lady should see to its being regulated, or this piece of furniture may do more harm than good. That good understanding which sometimes subsists between the clock and the cook, and which is brought about by the instrumentality of a broomhandle, or some such magic, should be noted by every provident housekeeper as one of the things to be guarded against.

If the cook's time-keeping was important, so too was the quality and taste of the dishes that she prepared. Employers liked their cook to follow proper recipes. There was a fear that if she relied on adding bits and pieces and then tasting every so often to see if the dish was right, the cook's taste buds would become insensible to all but strong flavours. This in turn would inevitably lead to odd-flavoured dishes appearing in the dining room – and it would be no good the mistress complaining, as the cook would not have a record of how much of each ingredient she had put in.

It is doubtful that many cooks did rely on written recipes for, unless a great change had been wrought by the first quarter of the twentieth century, kitchenmaids from that time tell me that the cooks they worked

Right: Cooks could sometimes be very trying

THE BRITISH DOMESTIC.
PHASE SECOND.—HER COOKERY.

"Don't want no cookery books, *I* don't. I could tell yer all wot's in 'em on my 'ead."

"Don't yewshewerly bile ribs o' beef in a fryin' pan, don't yer? P'r'aps yer'll teach yer granmother."

"Orternt to roast 'cod-fish on a string, orternt I? Diddent orter roast it at all, didn't I? Am I the cook or ain't I? Werry well!"

"Never see sich a dirty muck as things make yer hin! My fault, is it? Oh yus!"

"Tell yer wot it is—better git summun as *hain't* a minx! Better do it yerself—there! I'm ort—trubble yer for my next two year's wages—yah!"

under seldom looked at a recipe book and had their own terms for quantities. If, for example, a cook called for a 'nut' of butter, then the kitchenmaid knew that she wanted a piece the size of a walnut.

Professed cooks had learned their trade both by watching and by being left to learn by their own mistakes when they were kitchenmaids. Indeed, it was (I'm told) an irritation to kitchenmaids to be paid less than parlourmaids when their own job was more complicated by virtue of the many recipes they had to carry in their heads. Such recipes were hard-won, and cooks were often reluctant to part with them. This was amply illustrated as recently as the 1950s when the Queen Mother, staying at a house in Devon, told the cook how much she had enjoyed her asparagus ice and how she would love to know the recipe. The cook replied, 'Your late husband asked me that, ma'am, and I wouldn't give it to him.' And that was an end to the conversation.

In small households the cook generally described herself as a 'good plain cook'. She had less kitchen staff and did more cooking than her counterpart in a large establishment. In the smallest households the cook was known as a 'cook-general' and in addition to cooking she might also have to clean and sweep the front hall and front step and help lay up the dining room. It was these two types of cooks which presented mistresses with the most problems. Many were untrained, as good kitchenmaids who had worked in large houses rarely stooped to become cooks in small houses with no kitchenmaids to wait on them in turn. To make up for lack of experience some women bought instruction books. One publisher offered a whole set of these, ranging from *The Baker* to *The Varnisher*. Most were priced at a shilling but *The Cook* was 2 shillings and 6 pence.

Common to cooks in both middle-class and rich households were what were known as 'cook's perks'. There was beer money to help her cope with the heat of the kitchen, especially in summer, and money for her own pocket from selling dripping. Dripping was sold in the country to poor people who came to the back door and in the town to itinerant traders who resold it to shops. Beef dripping was the most common, as mutton fat set too hard. Rabbit skins, feathers and bones were also bought by rag-and-bone men. This back-door trading caused consternation to the economy-conscious mistress of lower middle-class houses. They feared a roaring trade in perfectly good items which could be reconstituted into meals for their own families. But preaching economy to some cooks was a lost cause, particularly those who, endeavouring to build up their stocks for selling, refused to cook with dripping and insisted instead on using the far more expensive butter. Mistresses could, however, get their own back with these rag-and-bone man deals, insisting that any money the cook got from him should go towards an object to adorn the kitchen,

The cook in her kitchen.
Kinnaird Castle, Angus

reasoning that, 'Many a little trifle may be obtained in this way, which, if not tending to give an air of luxury, will at least give some slight degree of comfort, and the maids will feel more pride in their room.'

Another perk regarded as an evil by employers was that of taking 'percentages'. This became so common that it was seen as a right and cooks refused to take jobs where they were not allowed them. The percentage system was worked with tradesmen who supplied the house with groceries, meat and fish. It was less prevalent in country houses where produce came from the estate. The cook did most of the ordering of goods from these tradesmen and the more she ordered from them the higher the percentage of the total cost they gave her to pocket personally. This inevitably led to her putting in large orders and the tradesmen charging the houseowner high prices in order to meet the percentages. The butler worked a similar system with the tradesmen he dealt with. The introduction of co-operative stores helped to curb this particular perk. Customers were required to pay cash, and masters and mistresses dealt with the stores directly rather than via a servant.

Perhaps a cook needed 'perks' to help her cope with old age. As late as 1880, professed cooks only earned £50 to £70 a year in quarterly instalments, whilst plain cooks earned £16 to £30.

The cook, then, was at the pinnacle of her profession. The unfortunate scullery maid, on the other hand, was so far below her that, figuratively speaking, she might have had to view her through a telescope.

In the 1860s scullery maids earned from £5 to £9 a year. By 1880 this had risen to between £12 and £18. Theirs was the lowliest job in the kitchen. Domestic work was viewed as good training for girls because it helped them manage their own homes when they got married; but kitchen work was known to be the hardest and most of the drudgery of kitchen work happened in the scullery. Despite this, parents from poor homes were only too glad to get their daughters jobs as scullery maids.

The cost of the journey from the girl's home to her place of employment was paid by the owner of the house she was going to. One girl who got a job as a scullery maid (and later became a cook in charge of a large kitchen) left home with a new tin box containing two new complete sets of underwear and two new working dresses. Her parents gave her 2/6d. and she was proud to tell her own children that she never asked for any financial help from that day onwards.

Girls were lucky if they got into a 'good' house where they were not mistreated and where servants' rations weren't short. They were lucky, too, if they had a clean comfortable bed. Most had to share with another kitchenmaid. Even if the mistress was kind, there were no luxuries. Carpet stopped dead where servants' quarters began and girls went from boiling hot kitchens up to icy bedrooms. Some mistresses made a point of visiting servants' rooms twice a year but steeled themselves to do so. They went with the preconceived idea that although their kitchens were kept beautiful, the kitchenmaids' own quarters could be a disgrace. A kind home gave a girl a good bed with washable dhurries laid beside it, a washstand and somewhere to hang her clothes. The girl's box, however, was not allowed to be kept in the room; it had to be locked away because it might tempt her to 'hoard rubbish'.

To be dressed properly, scullery maids had to have thick shoes or boots, an apron with a bib, a Holland apron and a dress with sleeves that could be rolled up. The dress would most likely have been of 'Oxford shirting'. It is uncertain what this material actually was, but even in its day it was thought of as ugly, if strong. Beneath the dress they wore stays, a flannel petticoat, a chemise, drawers and a flannel vest. Their hair had to be plaited and put up neatly under a cap.

Their duties lay mostly within the scullery adjoining the kitchen. Here they had to clean and scour stewpans, saucepans, sauté pans, frying pans and all the kitchen utensils. Mrs Pat Woolley of Leiston, Suffolk, recalls the kitchen in the big house where her aunt was employed as cook. She says that the scullery had 'two huge sinks, dank and dark, and what seemed

Right: Off to a job in service

Marian Gardiner

like hundreds of colanders and containers'. So large were some scullery sinks that girls had to stand on boxes in order to be able to reach inside them. Scullery maids also had to scrub floors and shelves and, often when few kitchenmaids were kept, to wash and prepare vegetables – but they were not to take them into the kitchen until asked to. In some big houses, vegetables were also cooked in the scullery – a worrying task as, with no means of controlling the temperature of the boilers, the vegetables either did not boil at all or boiled away to a pulp.

Plucking poultry and skinning game were also jobs which fell to the scullery maid. Quite literally fell, for on Mrs Crosby's first day (the lady who climbed 178 steps with cook's cup of tea) she saw at the scullery window which was below ground level, a man's two feet stop and then five rabbits and a hare were pushed through for her to skin. This apparently happened often and she had to rush across quickly to stop dead animals falling into the washing-up water in the sink.

A browse through any nineteenth-century cookery book will show that Victorians liked their fish and game to be served complete with its head still on, sometimes in macabre life-like poses. It was the scullery maid's task when skinning to quell as best she could a queasy stomach and gouge out the eyes of the rabbit or hare. This was something we unanimously agreed to leave out of the television series (as, in fact, we left out such delicacies as quails' eggs served in sheeps' ears and roast thrushes), but Ruth did show Alison the best way of plucking a pheasant. Although she did preface this by saying, 'I started my life plucking, I didn't intend finishing it in the same way, but anyhow....'

A very young servant girl

Apparently scullery maids' fingers soon got over their initial soreness from 'picking' birds. As Ruth said, when you've got fourteen to do in a morning you don't hang about. Young birds had to be picked low to extricate little quills at the base of their feathers. If this wasn't done the scullery maid might end up having to do the birds twice. Ruth said that teal were the worst birds to pick, such little things, all covered in down. She gave Alison the tip of feathering into a deep bucket, for if someone came to the scullery and opened the door the feathers were liable to be blown everywhere. It was, she said, trying to save yourself as much work as possible. Feathering was easier if a bird had been hung for 10 days, particularly if those days had been warmish and damp. Then the feathers almost dropped out – but so too did maggots, and there was the additional worry that the flesh tore easily.

Maggots could also get into the fat which scummed the sides of the oak metal-banded tubs in which washing-up was done. The fat had to be scraped off by hand and put into boxes, for someone would buy it at the back door and re-sell it for making soap.

Scullery maids started work at 6 o'clock in the morning in winter and 6.30 in the summer. If the mistress of the house liked to wash in rain water for the sake of her complexion, one of the first tasks was to boil sufficient for her so that she had it by 7 o'clock.

Days were long especially when dining hours got later. A scullery maid could still be washing pots and pans at 11 o'clock at night. In Ruth's early kitchen days this was not unusual. She described days when she got 'achy tired' and, shoes in her hand, took her clothes off as she went upstairs in a desperate effort to gain a few more minutes in bed. There were even some mornings when she woke up not in, but on the bed and still fully clothed from the night before.

Contact with home was by eagerly awaited letters. These arrived from the post office in a leather mail bag which went to the butler's pantry. The butler placed letters for kitchen staff on a special table. He sometimes delayed opening the bag, so despite frequent peering out of the kitchen door, the table remained bare.

After a year or eighteen months, a scullery maid stood the chance of being promoted. Promotion meant working in the kitchen as second kitchenmaid. Like the scullery maid, the second kitchenmaid rose at 6 o'clock. She did so in order to clean and light the kitchen range. In 1880 she could earn between £14 and £22 a year. One of a second kitchenmaid's most important duties was to lay the kitchen table up in the morning. This involved making sure that the brass dredgers kept in the middle of the table were full of flour and sugar, that the salt container was well supplied and that a plate of rough vegetables and herbs were available to the cook's hand if she wanted them for garnishing. She had to lay two boards either side of the table for the cook and head kitchenmaid to work on. Next to the cook's board she also had to place a white cloth and lay on that all the spoons and knives the cook would need for preparing and dishing-up breakfast. As each of these were used, they were rushed into the scullery to be washed. This lay-out of cook's spoons and knives was altered or added to for each meal.

Second kitchenmaids had to prepare flour, warm yeast till bubbling, get milk to the right temperature and grease tins so that the first kitchenmaid could bake bread. If the first kitchenmaid was busy, the second kitchenmaid made the bread herself. Bread was always made to be eaten the next day. In addition to ordinary loaves, a special one might have to be made for the 'family' breakfast. Instead of being baked this was put into a tin which fitted onto a revolving spit in front of the fire. It had to be watched in case the spit stopped turning and the bread burnt on one side.

The second kitchenmaid's duties might also include setting ice caves (see page 67) and doing all the roasting of meat. This was a job that demanded muscle. Catering for large households might mean carrying whole 'wings' of beef weighing up to as much as 50 lbs to a fire which got so hot that the surrounding flagstones were capable of burning the stitching in the soles of a kitchenmaid's boots. It needed muscle, too, to empty huge stockpots and carry copper pots full of vegetables. Ruth's doctor tells her that her shoulders are worn out. She says she's not surprised with the amount of heavy things she's carried in kitchens in the past, not to mention eels. It wasn't the weight of eels which affected her shoulders, but the way she had to skin them. It is, as every fisherman knows, notoriously difficult to kill eels but it was for the sake of freshness that they were brought live to the kitchen. More often than not, they were laid on a slab of ice in the fish larder until needed. Apparently many a new kitchenmaid sent to fetch an eel laid hands on the seemingly dead and stiff creature and then almost suffered a heart attack on the return journey when the eel, revived by the heat of her hands, began to wriggle frantically. Still alive, an eel was secured to a block with a fork and the skin around its neck split. This was then gripped tightly and pulled downwards until the whole of the eel's skin came off. It was this operation which contributed to Ruth's worn-out shoulders – so difficult was it to remove the skin.

Second kitchenmaids were in a good position to learn but they had to keep their eyes and ears open. When the approved menu slate returned from the mistress, it was hung in a prominent position in the kitchen. It might hang for an hour before being taken down. The kitchen staff then had to be able to inform cook exactly what was on the menu (if it was written in French, fear of the cook enhanced a maid's learning capacity) and what sauces and accompanying dishes were needed. If a kitchenmaid had a query on the garnish or sauce needed for a certain dish, it was the general rule that she was only told once. When that dish next reappeared on the menu she was expected to have remembered the correct things to accompany it. Careful kitchenmaids carried a stub of pencil and a scrap of paper to quickly write down what was said so that they didn't have the embarrassment of having to ask again. The learning process also involved being left to prepare a dish incorrectly from start to finish before being told that it was wrong. In this way the whole dish had to be done again from the beginning.

If the house held a large dinner party, a visiting chef might be called in and kitchenmaids could pick up tips from him. Another way of acquiring knowledge was for kitchenmaids to go to another big house where preparations were in hand for a grand dinner party and to help out. Similarly they could go to hotels. Before the last war if you paid the chef at the Savoy 5 or 10 shillings, he would allow you to watch him work.

Servants at Hanham Hall, Suffolk, posing for a group photograph in 1883

After two or three years, a second kitchenmaid could try to better herself by applying for the job of first kitchenmaid in another house. In his 1840 edition of *The Cook's Oracle*, Dr William Kitchiner described the first kitchenmaid (or second cook, as she was also known) as having the hardest place in the house and being the worst paid. She did, he said, truly verify the old adage, 'the more work, the less wages.'

According to *The Servants' Practical Guide*, published in 1880, a first kitchenmaid was earning £20 to £28 a year. She had to be in the kitchen by 7 o'clock each morning. Trussing poultry, making ice creams, making sauces and preparing different dishes under the cook's direction were part of her duties. In seniority, she was one step down from the cook and she did all the plain cooking required for the dining room. She also cooked for the school room and nursery. Not the least of her burdens was that she also had to cook for all the servants (in later years the second kitchenmaid took on this task) who could be quite as fussy as the dining room. Servants' meals were complicated and formal, revolving around who ate where and which servant waited on which.

In very grand houses where there was a house steward, the upper servants – that is, the butler, the housekeeper, the cook, the valet, the lady's maid and the nurse – ate with the steward in his room. They were waited on by the steward's boy, who could use the experience to train as a footman. Where there was no steward, they ate in the housekeeper's room. Whichever room was used, it was always referred to as 'The Room' by the lower servants or, less respectfully, as 'Pugs' Parlour'.

Footmen, housemaids, still-room maids and perhaps grooms and the odd job man ate in the servants' hall, a room with long scrubbed tables and benches. The kitchenmaids had their meals in the kitchen. If they were busy they ate when they could, a favourite evening dish being ribs of lamb dipped in salt. If they sat down to a meal, the first kitchenmaid always sat at the head of the table. The scullery maid often had to eat in the servants' hall so that she could see when one course was finished and run and get the next course for everyone. This often meant she had to eat her food quickly. Servants brought by house guests went, depending on their status, to 'The Room' or the servants' hall. As Ruth said, there were three lots of meals downstairs before you ever got to the dining room and, if there was a nursery in the house, another lot on the next floor.

Mealtime in the servants' hall

Servants' breakfast time was 8 o'clock in summer and half past 8 in winter. In the housekeeper's room, the still-room maid put a cloth on the table and laid out the cutlery. Breakfast here could consist of cold meats like ham or cold roast beef or boiled pork, bacon and eggs, toast, butter and preserves. The housekeeper poured the tea and the butler carved the meat. In the servants' hall, the head housemaid poured, the under-butler carved, people sat in strict order of precedence and the younger servants were not allowed to speak unless spoken too. The usual hall breakfast was cold meat and bread and butter, they rarely had bacon and eggs. Tables were cleared by the lowest servants, who set them again for lunch at 11 o'clock.

Lunch was cold meat and beer or, in smaller houses, bread and cheese and beer. A considerable amount of beer seems to have been consumed by Victorian servants, particularly the men. They were entitled to a pint at lunch, a pint at dinner, and a pint at supper. Women could have half a pint at lunch, a pint at dinner and half a pint at supper but, despite beer being seen as 'a healthy tonic, promoting digestion and increasing circulation', many women preferred to have money in lieu. The custom of giving beer money was still in force as recently as forty years ago, when it was 6d. a day. Mrs Gwen Lavers of Millbrook in Cornwall told me that she was unfortunate enough to have an employer who was friendly with the brewing family, Bass. This meant that beer was supplied instead of beer money and the staff had to fight to get their beer money reinstated. Money in lieu in Victorian times, and I suppose in later years the thinking was still the same, was seen to give less incentive for idlers to hang around the kitchen in the expectation of a free pint. Not giving beer did have one disadvantage, particularly in town houses. It gave the men servants an excuse to pop out to the nearest public house. In the country this wasn't always possible, but country butlers generally brewed their own beer — perhaps just as well, as public house beer was often adulterated with sugar, treacle, salt and tobacco. The half dozen or so upper servants, with presumably more refined tastes, were allowed between them four bottles of wine a week.

According to *The Servants' Practical Guide*, the main meal of the day, dinner, was served at 1 o'clock. Both upper and lower servants dined at the same table in the servants' hall. However, after the first course of hot meat and vegetables, the upper servants withdrew to have their sweet and bread and cheese in the housekeeper's room. A choice of sweets was expected there and puddings or tarts were placed opposite the housekeeper whilst the still-room maid handed round the plates. She then ran back to finish her own dinner but when 'The Room' bell was rung had to return with the bread and cheese.

Tea took place between 4 and 5. All the upper servants except the cook had tea in 'The Room'. Meanwhile in the kitchen the cook put a white cloth on the table, poured the tea and presided over bread and butter, dry toast and plum cake. During servants' mealtimes considerate employers tried to remember not to ring their own bells. Perhaps as much for the employers as for the servants themselves, a bell was rung to announce all servants' meals, except tea.

The final meal, supper, was served at 8 or 9 o'clock in the evening. In 'The Room', the upper servants might dress for supper. They had a hot meal with the addition of entrées and sweets sent down from the dining room. Some economic mistresses only allowed the left-over joints to be eaten, expecting any uneaten entrées and sweets to reappear at dining-room luncheon the next day. Servants in the hall had cold meat, hot vegetables and bread and cheese. In small houses they might only have cold meat and bread and cheese, and some did not even have meat.

If the family was away, the servants left in the house were given board wages each week. The maximum given for men in 1880 was 16 shillings and for women, 14 shillings. This enabled them to buy their own food. If the kitchen staff were away with the family, the other servants never entered the kitchen but cooked their food on a range in the servants' hall.

Many servants had food in variety and quality that they would never have been able to afford in their own homes. In the lower middle-class houses owned by people trying to keep up appearances despite slender incomes, it wasn't such a happy story. Mistresses were obliged to augment the kitchen's meagre diet with the occasional jar of potted meat or preserve in order to stop them pilfering food delicacies intended for upstairs. One lady, contributing to a article on the subject of cheap dinners, wrote to the *Fish Traders Gazette* in 1883, saying: 'I always have a fish dinner once a week for my servants; the fishmonger has standing orders to send 1s 6d worth of fish every Wednesday; this provides dinner for four healthy servants with keen appetites.' The fish in question must have been as miraculous as its biblical counterpart (although she makes no mention of loaves), for the lady continued: 'I also partake of the fish for my luncheon, and there is usually quite enough left over for breakfast for my husband and myself next morning.'

As a general rule, late Victorian household accounts were calculated on the figures that it cost £30 a year to keep a man servant in food (including the beer he consumed) and between £20 and £25 to feed a woman servant. Sometimes less for women, for it appeared that a few female servants seemed to live on air, although they were acknowledged as rare exceptions. Perhaps the poor maid-of-all-work came nearest to this description, for she was supposed to live on little more than 'the leavings of the table.'

Left: A housemaid (top) and scullerymaid (bottom) dressed in their best and photographed by their mistress

If the cost of keeping a servant worried an employer, the cost of keeping themselves worried the servants. Kitchen staff along with other servants were often expected to pay for their own tea and sugar. The cost of half a pound of tea per month and half a pound of sugar a week, added to the cost of buying new clothes and shoes, left little over from their wages. Yet living in a generation of people suffused with the ideals of 'Self-Help', 'Thrift' and 'Character', servant girls were told it was their duty to save. In 1861 the post office started up savings banks and if a girl gave tuppence over the counter she would be given back a book divided into twelve squares. It was hoped that the ten empty squares would weigh on her

Below: Housekeeper and domestic servants, 1886

conscience until she'd passed further tuppences over the counter. When the book was filled she'd be given another empty one and so *ad infinitum*.

If she started saving when she first went into service at the age of 12 or 13, by the time she was 26 a young woman might have amassed (with the help of interest at 6d. per sovereign per annum) £100. One of the reasons urged on a girl to save was so that she could support those dependent on her. This is given an odd twist by a story told to me by a lady whose mother was a kitchenmaid at the turn of the century:

Just before Christmas on one of her rare half days her mistress must have got to hear she was going near some shops; so she asked my mother to purchase a packet of tea for her but produced no money to pay for the tea. My mother had no cash but was too proud to inform her mistress of this or ask help of the other servants. She took her precious Post Office Savings Book to the Post Office and asked for five shillings. This was to be her first withdrawal and she had no knowledge as to what action she had to take. The assistant, busy with the Christmas rush, was anything but helpful when my mother asked for help in completing the withdrawal form. My mother was made to feel so small in front of all the Christmas shoppers. That packet of tea was one of the most difficult purchases of her life.

She had started work at £8 a year, and set herself the target of earning £100 a year. She finally achieved this in 1926.

Any girl practising such thrift was to be encouraged by her mistress, who should show that she approved of the girl not wasting her money on 'finery'. One tangible way of doing this was for her to occasionally give the girl one of her own ribbons or bestow on her a suitable bonnet. Not only would this nurture the thrift habit, but it would guard against the mistress's artistic feelings being outraged by any vulgar glaring colour the girl might have bought!

It is to be hoped that such ribbons didn't make the girls too attractive for, in well-ordered households, 'followers' (boyfriends) were strictly forbidden. Followers were looked on as being liable to steal things from the kitchen and had a habit of hanging around for free food and beer. They could cause the mistress of the house undue worry. In fact, a book advising husbands on the care of their wives during the critical three-week period after the birth of a baby, warned that such news as 'Cook has had a soldier to tea' might cause the wife to have a severe setback.

Small households relaxed the no male visitors rule, providing that permission was always asked first. The servant was also required to tell her mistress the name of the visitor and his relationship to her.

Close familiarity between the men and women house servants was forbidden. Male servants' bedrooms were as far removed as possible from the women's sleeping quarters. However, as Victorian agony aunt Mrs Panton had said, 'Servants have their feelings and passions as strong as,

The arrival of the postman presented an interesting diversion from dreary kitchen chores

or perhaps often stronger than their masters, and they will indulge them somehow or other'. If this indulgence resulted in a kitchenmaid becoming pregnant the father, if he was a fellow servant, was sacked. The girl was also given her notice and taken to the local workhouse to have the child.

Many kitchenmaids married gardeners or gamekeepers employed on the estate whose work brought them into contact with the kitchen. Cooks and housekeepers were rarely married but they were always given the courtesy title 'Mrs'. Employers preferred their butlers, too, to be unmarried, as having a wife and family would mean that the butler could have divided loyalties, not be smartly dressed and be tempted to filch provisions and drink. He might also, heaven forbid, be tempted to pawn the household silver placed under his care if his family got into debt. There was little doubt that the butler, if so inclined, had every opportunity for spiriting things away and sometimes temptation did prove too difficult to resist. Mrs Crosby of Stroud told me that a housemaid colleague cleaning the dining-room curtains had found, folded inside them and wrapped in a napkin, several succulent slices of ham. The curtains had obviously proved a useful lodging place until the butler could remove the ham unobserved.

One relationship that employers did foster was that between their servants and God. At 8.30 each morning, after the servants' breakfast was over, the cook was required to lead her kitchen staff into the upstairs dining room to join the other servants for morning prayers. Prayers were read by the master of the house or, in his absence, by the mistress. The children of the family also came down from the nursery. Everyone had to kneel for prayers. The usual arrangement was to rest one's elbows on the dining-room chairs which were set back from the table. A lady of considerable age and who has sadly since died, told me that as a child she always tried to pick a chair near a window, so that she could amuse herself by peering through the chair back at what was happening outside. Prayers lasted for fifteen minutes. The servants filed out and the family sat down to breakfast. Gardeners whose duty it was to do the floral decorations in the house had an uncanny knack of missing prayers by about ten minutes.

In addition to morning prayers, servants were expected to attend church once every Sunday and twice every other Sunday, either morning or afternoon, whichever fitted in best with their work. In church they had to sit in pews which were specially allocated for them. The unwritten rule of church attendance carried on until well into living memory. Women who had worked as scullery and kitchenmaids told me that they were allowed half a day a week off in the week and all day every alternate Sunday. But as they were expected to go to church, they ended up with just half a day free on Sunday.

Their mid-week half day started when the lunchtime washing-up was finished and, providing that the cook didn't find them an extra job to do, they could be away by 2.30 pm but had to be back by 9 o'clock that evening. On their return they often finished the day by rolling up their sleeves and helping the weary scullery maid finish her piles of washing-up. If their hours away from the kitchen seem frugal, their mothers and grandmothers had even less free time. They were allowed one afternoon a week and a whole day only once a month. If a girl's parents lived within walking distance, she could go home on her day off. Walking distance in the country might be a dozen miles or more, and when darkness fell a member of her family would have to walk part of the way back with her. To get over the difficulty of having someone to walk back with, particularly in winter when darkness fell early, some kitchenmaids came to arrangements with parlourmaids. If their day off fell on the same day both would go to the parlourmaid's home and the next day off both would go to the kitchenmaid's home. It meant seeing their own families less but ensured company on the return journey. Lady's maids fared even worse than kitchen staff. Although they were allowed some free time in the afternoon, albeit probably exercising their mistress's dog, they were never allowed whole holidays because it would inconvenience their mistress too much.

Men servants had more freedom. The butler was allowed to go out every morning from 12 until 1 and again from half past 9 to 11 at night. Footmen, too, if not required after dinner, could go out but also had to be back by 11 o'clock.

Right: Away from the confines of the house, servant girls could fall prey to masculine attention

Not all employers were unfeeling when it came to servants' free time. In 1878, Dr and Mrs Delamere published an interesting book entitled *Wholesome Fare – a Sanitary Cook-Book*. Its main aim is to attack the excesses of Victorian eating habits and provide healthy alternatives, but there is a section in the book given over to cold Sunday and other holiday dinners. By adopting these the Delameres say that employers can take up as little of the kitchen's time as possible. A recommended dinner menu for Ash Wednesday is shown right. All the food could be prepared in advance and, if necessary, heated up on the day.

Despite the restrictions on free time, the number of women working in a kitchen must have generated its own social camaraderie and truly social occasions did take place for servants in large houses. These took the form of suppers and balls at Christmas, Twelfth Night or the coming-of-age of the family son and heir. In the servants' hall, cleared and decorated, the master of the house led off the dancing with the housekeeper followed by the mistress with the butler. But even with kitchen and

Common Soup Maigre
Boiled Salt Cod
Egg Sauce
Parsnips
Matelote of Poached Eggs
Stewed celery, white
Eels in Jelly
Salad
Welsh Rabbits

THE SERVANTS' BALL.
(Of course Patronised by the Family.)

scullery maids becoming cinderellas for the night, one wonders who spent hours during the day preparing the following Supper Menu given for a Household Ball at Madresfield Court in August 1893:

Soup
Consommé

Gros Pièces	*Entremets*
Salmon Mayonnaise au Gridoni	Trifles aux Cupidons
Raised Pâté Pigeons and Mushrooms	Tipsy Cake · Jelly with Fruits
Beef à la Mode en Jelly	Pineapple Cream
York Ham décoré	Charlotte Russe · Jelly Marasquin
Ox Tongue à la Macédoine	Gâteau Mould
Lamb and Mint Sauce	Meringues with Cream
Chicken with Cresses	
Lobster Salad	Cakes, Fruits, Rolls &c.

The social calendar of their masters and mistresses also brought a sort of social life for some kitchen servants. At certain times of the year the family would move from the country to their town house and vice versa, taking with them a complement of servants. If the entourage travelled by train, the family went, of course, first class, whilst the kitchen staff went second. The staff took with them a small spirit lamp on which to make a cup of tea, hampers containing the provisions they would need in the house they were going to and the family silver, carried by the head footman or under-butler.

One hopes that such Victorian staff journeys went more smoothly than some of those undertaken by the next generation. I was told stories of a footman who forgot to bring the silver to the station and kept the train waiting whilst he went back to get it, of kitchenmaids getting tipsy mid-journey on a bottle of homemade wine and Ruth admits to trying to disown a hamper on Kings Cross Station. In the hamper, packed beneath cakes and food, a bag of pearl barley had burst. A steady trickle of pearl barley issuing through the bottom of the hamper delighted hundreds of pigeons. They settled in a long line behind the porter as he progressed along the platform with Ruth, who was trying to pretend that she wasn't part of the interesting spectacle.

Birds seem to have had a habit of blighting Ruth's attempts at life outside the kitchen. When she was with her employers at their home in Scotland she occasionally sneaked out in the evening to dances. When she left she slid down the bannister rail to avoid the alarming creaks the stairs could make. Her return at 4 or 5 in the morning was rather more tricky. Ruth always asked the footman who slept near the silver safe to let her in if she tapped on his window. Despite taking care not to scrunch on any gravel, however, the minute she set foot inside the grounds of the house, all the peacocks would screech and squawk. This necessitated nipping in, as Ruth said, 'a bit sudden', and knowing that a combination of peacock screeches and creaking stairs would wake the whole house she had to get back to her room by hauling herself up the bannister rail, hand over fist.

An 'overworked' cook and housemaid discuss their lot

SERVANTGALISM.—No. II.

Housemaid. "WELL, SOOSAN, I'VE MADE UP MY MIND NOT TO STOP 'ERE NO LONGER TO WORK LIKE NEGROES AS WE DO!"

Cook. "NOR I, NUTHER! BUT JUST TURN THE MEAT, WILL YOU, PLEASE, THE WHILST I FINISH MY CROCHET?"

CHAPTER FOUR
Kitchen Fittings

. . . a good cook will scarcely be able to do justice to her powers unless she is
allowed to have a proper and sufficient kitchen range with other requisites presently
to be detailed.

ooking in the eighteenth century was done on a fire set into
an open grate, the fire being controlled by moving the sides
of the grate to make it bigger or smaller. Pots and kettles were
suspended over the fire on swinging iron bars fixed to the side of the
fireplace. Some, called recons, had a piece of iron attached to them and
pots could be raised or lowered by putting hooks of varying lengths into
holes punched into the piece of iron. Bread was cooked in an oven beside
the fireplace and meat roasted on spits. The spits were turned either by a
wind-up mechanism or by smoke jacks. A smoke jack fitted into the
chimney. It was a horizontal wheel filled with metal spokes set obliquely
like the sails of a windmill. The spokes turned when a current of hot air
and smoke hit them, in turn rotating another wheel to which a chain was
attached. The chain stretched down to a wheel fastened to the spit, and
so the spit rotated. The hotter the fire, the faster the jack went round.
Smoke jacks were seldom used in small houses because they were so noisy,
a particular embarrassment if the dining room was over the kitchen.

Towards the end of the eighteenth century, the Industrial Revolution
began to pave the way for the cast-iron ranges which were to dominate
Victorian kitchens. Mechanisation in the mines made coal more easily
available; a way was found to perfect the making of cast iron; and the
growth of railways helped to transport salesmen, ranges, and (if the
purchaser would pay the second-class fares) range fitters, to most parts of
the country.

Early ranges were called 'open' because the fire was not enclosed. The
first open range was designed by Thomas Robinson in 1780. It had an
oven on one side of the fire grate and a tank for hot water on the other
side. It also had a drawback: food on the side nearest to the fire burnt
easily. The invention of flues to carry heat around the oven went some
way towards making it more efficient.

The larger the household the bigger the open range. Meat was still
roasted in front of the range on a horizontal spit worked by a smoke jack.
In smaller houses, however, a joint was roasted by suspending it from a

hook fastened to a line which was in turn fastened to a bottle jack. The jack, a bottle-shaped metal device with a clockwork mechanism inside, was hung from the mantelpiece. Once wound up the jack would rotate the joint first one way, then the other. Ruth showed Alison how to use a bottle jack. It soon became clear that the jack had to be kept an eye on as it frequently needed re-winding. Another danger was that if the fire was uneven the joint cooked at the top and not the bottom.

The open range was followed by the closed range. Although patented in 1802 this did not become widely used until the middle of the century. It was called 'closed' (or 'enclosed') because an iron plate blocked the heat from going up the chimney and diverted it instead into a series of flues which went behind and warmed the ovens. Closed ranges were also known as 'kitcheners'. They were considered to make more efficient use of coal, even if they did consume more coal because air from the kitchen had to pass through the fire before passing into the chimney.

Due to the smaller expanse of exposed fire on closed ranges, the method of roasting with a bottle jack had to be modified. A semi-circular screen which could be stood directly in front of the fire was manufactured. The screen was made of polished tin and a bottle jack could be hung on a handle at the top of it. Half enclosed and with the shiny metal helping to reflect the heat, a joint attached to the jack quickly roasted. Not surprisingly, these screens were known as 'hasteners'. So that the screen did not have to be moved away from the fire in order to baste the meat inside, a door was cut into the back. Through this a kitchenmaid could baste the joint by scooping up fat caught in a well at the base of the screen.

Many closed ranges were totally enclosed, the fire not being visible at all. This meant that the ovens had to be specially ventilated to take off the noxious fumes that people feared meat, particularly venison, contained. Although 'funeral baked' meat (large quantities) was accepted, the relative merits of cooking meat or roasting it in front of a fire, had been a matter of dispute for years. Many people, perhaps thinking back to the times when their meat had been cooked, sometimes unsatisfactorily, in the local baker's oven, swore by open-fire roasting.

Towards the end of the eighteenth century a philanthropist and inventor named Count Romford was so horrified by the amount of coal wasted in open-fire roasting that he invented an enclosed 'roaster'. He exhibited it at the Royal Institution, a place set up to allow people to see new inventions and improvements. The roaster was a cylinder of sheet iron, 18 inches wide and 24 inches high, with a hinged door. The cylinder was set horizontally into a wall, with the door flush with the front of the brick-work. Beneath it a fire sent hot air to a network of iron flues around the cylinder. The joint was placed above a drip pan. To stop the heat from the

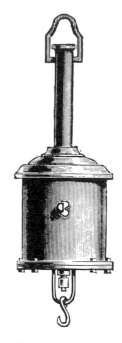

Bottle jack

Alison helps Ruth put the meat hastener to use

A fuel-saving 'kitchener' of 1887

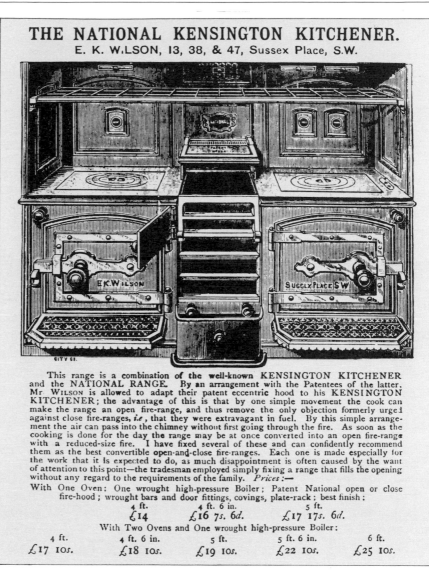

THE NATIONAL KENSINGTON KITCHENER.
E. K. WILSON, 13, 38, & 47, Sussex Place, S.W.

This range is a combination of the well-known KENSINGTON KITCHENER and the NATIONAL RANGE. By an arrangement with the Patentees of the latter, Mr WILSON is allowed to adapt their patent eccentric hood to his KENSINGTON KITCHENER; the advantage of this is that by one simple movement the cook can make the range an open fire-range, and thus remove the only objection formerly urged against close fire-ranges, *i.e*, that they were extravagant in fuel. By this simple arrangement the air can pass into the chimney without first going through the fire. As soon as the cooking is done for the day the range may be at once converted into an open fire-range with a reduced-size fire. I have fixed several of these and can confidently recommend them as the best convertible open-and-close fire-ranges. Each one is made especially for the work that it is expected to do, as much disappointment is often caused by the want of attention to this point—the tradesman employed simply fixing a range that fills the opening without any regard to the requirements of the family. *Prices :—*

With One Oven: One wrought high-pressure Boiler; Patent National open or close fire-hood; wrought bars and door fittings, covings, plate-rack; best finish:

4 ft.	4 ft. 6 in.	5 ft.
£14	£16 7s. 6d.	£17 17s. 6d.

With Two Ovens and One wrought high-pressure Boiler:

4 ft.	4 ft. 6 in.	5 ft.	5 ft. 6 in.	6 ft.
£17 10s.	£18 10s.	£19 10s.	£22 10s.	£25 10s.

bottom of the cylinder burning the fat when it dropped into the drip pan, the pan was made up of two plates with a space in between and water was poured into the space (interestingly, Shrewsbury's Portable Gas Oven, manufactured almost a century later, had a drip pan of identical design).

Romford tested the roaster at the Foundling Institution of London. He roasted 112 lbs of beef using only 22 lbs of coal valued at 3 pence (coal was then 25 shillings a ton). In addition to being economical, Romford claimed that meat roasted in his roaster was 'better tasted, higher flavoured and much more juicy and delicate than when roasted on a spit before an open fire'.

The roaster was, however, short-lived as the iron piping which carried the hot air around the cylinder soon burnt out and crumbled. Romford modified the design in another invention which he called a 'roasting oven'. In this the air was not heated by flames coming directly into contact with the iron flues. Instead the air was heated by passing along the hot base of the oven and then rising up through an outlet behind. Although not as effective as his original design, Romford believed his sort of roasting oven would become widely used. Towards the end of the nineteenth century, Romford's prophecy was amply borne out – closed kitcheners were being fitted in 90 per cent of all newly built houses and the need to give special ventilation to the oven designated for roasting meat had been forgotten.

Ranges had intriguing trade names. There was 'Lodger', 'Thrift', 'Livingstone', 'Stanley' and even one called 'Conqueror'. The latter must have seemed aptly named to a kitchenmaid as she crept downstairs at 6 o'clock each morning preparing to battle in the cold and dark to get the range ready for its day's work.

First of all she had to rake out the spent ashes. Any cinders left had to be separated from the ashes as they could still burn, and careful mistresses drummed into their kitchenmaids that it was wasteful and wicked to throw away cinders. One day a week the kitchenmaid had to come down at 5 o'clock in order to clean out the flues. Ruth recalls having to get the

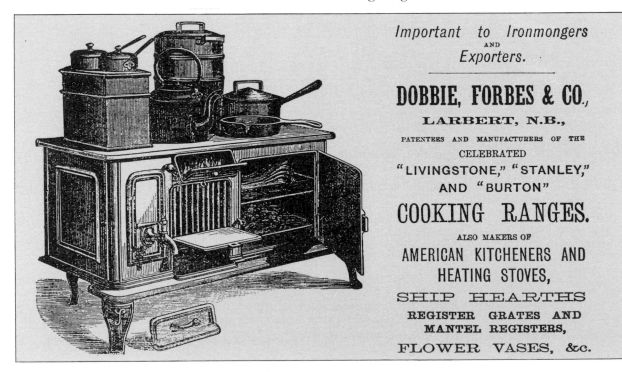

watchman, who patrolled the house at night with a dog, to wake her so that she'd be up in time.

If the flues were blocked with soot, air could not flow through them and the oven would not heat. This could have a marginal benefit for if one flue was left sooted-up it formed a crude method of heat control, the kitchenmaid knowing that there was one hot oven and one cool one. But as a rule all flues needed to be swept. There were a variety of ingenious devices to help in this filthy job. The most straightforward was a long narrow brush with a bent handle. If you didn't have that you could use a long chain tied to a stick – rattling the chain inside the flue dislodged the soot, and pulling the chain raked it out. An old toasting fork tied to a piece of string with a weight at one end surrounded with straw, served the same purpose. 'The Wizard' cooking range, invented in 1880, had flue scrapers built into its design. The makers claimed that by pulling the handles attached to the scrapers, the flues could be cleaned without 'soiling the hands'. 'The Wizard' must have had a defect somewhere, for it didn't seem to catch on; and as long as ranges were in use, the chore of cleaning the flues remained. So dirty did a kitchen maid become that when she finished she had to carry water up the many flights of stairs to her room and wash before she could come back down to help make breakfast.

Even on the days the flues didn't have to be cleaned, the process of getting the range ready was still a dirty job. After sticks, paper and wood had been laid into the grate, black lead had to be applied to its iron body. The black lead (which was a mixture of carbon and iron) was purchased in sticks. It was mixed with a little drop of turpentine and then put on a brush in the same way as shoe polish. One brush had to be used to put it on, another to brush it off, and another to bring up a shine. If the range

Alison discovers the dubious pleasures of black-leading

was still warm from the night before, the shine came up much more quickly. Black lead was never put on to the top of the range where the pots and kettles stood.

Any steel on the range also had to be burnished. Glove-shaped pieces of leather with fine chain on one side could be worn to do this. Ruth never needed these gloves. She used to deal with steel plates on ranges by simply removing them on sight and hiding them in a cupboard. This gave the range, in her opinion, a pleasing uncluttered look and was, she believed, a far better system than cleaning them.

After the fiddly flint and tinder box, the invention of matches in the 1830s must have been a blessing. Lucifer matches were small sticks of wood tipped with a paste containing phosphorus. When lit the matches smelt strongly of sulphuric acid and a lady in her nineties told me she remembers people sniffing sulphur matches, rather like some people sniff glue today.

Burnished, brushed and with its best face to the world, the range could be difficult. Wind – or rather the lack of it – was often the problem. Once the fire was going well in the grate a scuttle of coal had to be put on and the flue dampers kept open so that the fire worked up to a white-hot heat. This was simple enough, but once the dampers were pushed in to divert heat to the ovens, if the wind was in a certain direction the fire would go out. A trying event when the kitchenmaid was endeavouring to get the ovens hot enough for the cook to use when she appeared at 5 minutes to 8. Ruth's solution, she said, was to speak nicely to the footmen in the pantry. They changed the candles on the dining-room table every day and would let her have the candlestubs. These quickly set the fire ablaze.

The temperature inside the ovens of early ranges was often an unknown quantity. A firm called Joseph Davis invented a thermometer which could be attached to the oven door so that the bulb was inside and the tube with mercury in it outside. This made it possible to read the temperature without opening the door. Joseph Davis also made a thermometer which could be stood inside the oven. But such refinements were rare and kitchen staff generally had their own methods of testing the heat. One was to sprinkle a pinch of flour on to the floor of the oven. If the flour went brown, the oven was nicely hot; if it went black, it was too hot. Another way was the paper method. The following instructions came from Mr Black's *Household Cookery*:

1 If a sheet of paper burns when thrown in, the oven is too hot.
2 When the paper becomes dark brown, it is suitable for pastry.
3 When light brown, it does pies.
4 When dark yellow, for cakes.
5 When light yellow, for puddings, biscuits, and small pastry.

If the household had no still room, cakes had to be baked in the kitchen oven. This was generally done in the afternoon when the heat had died down. To make doubly sure that a cake did not burn on the bottom, the cake tin was set into a tray filled with 3 inches of sand. This method had a therapeutic by-product: cooks whose long years of kitchen service had left them with rheumaticky hands could relieve the aching by plunging their hands into the warm sand and letting it trickle through their fingers.

Large ranges consumed prodigious quantities of coal. The fire had to be fierce for early morning grilling and toasting, and when the dining-room breakfast had been taken in it had to be made up once more. Coal was again added after luncheon so that it would be hot enough for kettles at teatime. Another major refuelling happened before dinner was cooked. It wasn't unusual for twelve large scuttles to be emptied during the day. At Chirk Castle in North Wales, the massive open range (still in use in the 1930s when Lord and Lady Howard de Walden were lavishly entertaining) burnt 5 cwt of coal a day.

With its attendant agonies of cleaning, fuelling and controlling, it is surprising that the coal range lasted out for so long against its rival, the gas range. In 1850, James Sharp of Southampton was the first firm to offer a gas range for sale. Three years prior to this an Act of Parliament had been passed regulating the supply of gas to the public and gas lighting was becoming widespread.

There was, however, general reluctance to use gas for cooking. People believed that food roasted or baked over gas jets would become impregnated with the noxious vapours. (This is perhaps hardly surprising at a time when ladies were being told that the ordinary biological gases given off from lungs and bodies in a crowded room, could have devastating effects. These effects would be apparent on their faces should they be so bold as to wear make-up. The gases would turn their complexions the colour of lead and, if they were foolhardy enough to remain any length of time, their faces would turn quite black.)

The dangers of exposing food to coal gas were somewhat lessened in 1868. In that year a Mr Shrewsbury invented Shrewsbury's Portable Gas Oven. Instead of the gas jets being near the food, he placed them beneath the oven. The heat from the jet rose around the outside and top of the oven and any gas fumes were dispelled through an outlet. At the top of Mr Shrewsbury's gas oven there was a hotplate and he was able to boast that the oven could carry out mulifarious modes of cooking, all at the same time. The nether jets could grill, toast or bake, the oven roast and the hotplate boil.

The obvious benefits of cooking on gas ranges gradually became apparent and dispelled the prejudices against them. With gas there was no need to carry coals or clean flues, the temperature could easily be regulated, the bases of cooking pots did not become blackened as they did on coal ranges, and food could be heated instantly, at any time of the day or night, which was particularly useful if you were looking after a baby or an invalid.

The popularity of gas cooking was heavily promoted by the gas companies. Gas ranges were hired out for a small rent and penny-in-the-slot meters introduced. By the 1880s, cookery books were including recipes tailored to suit gas stoves. In her book *Domestic Cookery: with special reference to Cooking by Gas*, Miss H. M. Young (First Class Diplomee as Demonstrator of Cookery, Medallist, &c. &c.) makes much of the 'Convenience, Cleanliness and Economy' of gas. She worked out that with gas then priced at 3s. 6d. per 1000 feet, the whole of the cooking for a middle-class family could be done at a cost not exceeding $2\frac{1}{2}$d. a day, whereas to do the same on a coal range would cost 7d. to one shilling a day. If women needed further convincing, then Miss Young, a doughty economist, tells us that a 10 lb joint reduces to 6 lbs when cooked in a coal range, but when cooked by gas eventually weighs in at $7\frac{1}{2}$ lbs. She argues that the cost of the difference of this instance alone would cover the cost of the gas.

Early gas cookers were made of heavy iron, and it was recommended that instead of standing on a wooden floor they be placed onto a sheet of iron or slab of slate. Gas ranges were manufactured to suit various needs. There was, for example, one with a gas water boiler attached so that water could be heated without lighting the main range. Coal grates were attached to the side of others. The coal grate being used in the winter with the added benefit of warming the kitchen and in the heat of the summer, the gas part alone being used.

To a generation raised on the drudgery of cleaning coal ranges, the instructions issued for cleaning a gas cooker were remarkably simple – wipe out the interior if it was enamelled and if not, limewash the oven occasionally. But old habits died hard, and a special instruction had to be added telling women not to black lead the burners as this clogged the jets.

Despite this, and the fact that many large mansions used gas for lighting and often had their own gas-making machines, coal ranges continued to dominate the big kitchens until well into this century. In some places a gas oven was used as a back-up.

As a smelly footnote, Ruth remembers being instructed to cook on chicken gas. Her employer had droppings from his hen houses converted into gas and piped to the kitchen. Any Victorian objections to noxious fumes would have been amply founded in this case. When droppings were scarce, to the general relief of the kitchen, coal gas was resumed.

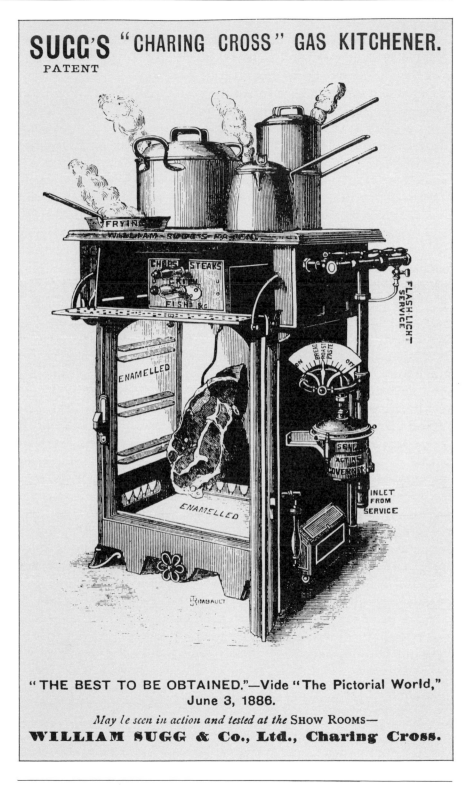

An advertisement in the 1887 edition of High-class Cookery Recipes *by Mrs Charles Clarke*

Kingpin though the range was in the Victorian kitchen, it was only one of a whole battery of utensils and devices necessary for the gastronomic well-being of gentry and house servants.

In addition to the range, many large establishments had stewing pans, which were rows of hotplates heated by burning charcoal in alcoves beneath. These stoves were invaluable for keeping pots gently simmering. The kitchenmaid could also use them to cook her vegetables if the range was crowded. Their usefulness, however, was countered by their dangers – the burning charcoal gave off carbonic acid or choke-damp. To counteract this, one or two shallow dishes filled with water and sprinkled with lime were placed nearby before the charcoal was lit. The idea was that the lime would attract the carbonic acid and form carbonate of lime which would collect on the surface of the water. The carbonate of lime could be skimmed off several times before the lime content of the water was exhausted. Ruth remembers using charcoal stewing pans but not the makeshift purifiers. She believes that it was the big, draughty kitchens which kept kitchen staff from expiring and that charcoal only became obsolete when kitchens got smaller and better insulated!

If charcoal stoves presented dangers, so, too, could the placing and fitting of various fitments around the ordinary range. Huge dripping pans, some almost 4 foot by 2½ foot, were brought out and set before the fire each morning. Fat from spit-roasting meat dripped into the pan. The meat was often wrapped in paper tied like a parcel and as it rotated the hot fat was scooped with a huge ladle and trickled over it. The combination of hot fat, fire and paper, often set the paper alight – and sometimes the kitchenmaid with it. If these dangers could be avoided there was still the hazardous task of emptying the boiling fat out of the dripping tray into big basins. This needed a kitchenmaid either end of the driptray.

Above: Basting tray and ladle

Below: Braising pan and gridiron

Close proximity to burning coals was sometimes a distinct possibility for kitchenmaids working in a grand house. For (although used by some English cooks) the method of cooking meat with a braising pan, was practised more by French chefs. Meat with broth and vegetables was put into the pan and the lid placed on and sealed round with clay or dough. The pan was then placed on the corner of the range to simmer. The tricky part came next. Live embers and hot ashes had to be tansferred from the range fire into the concave top of the lid. E. S. Dallas, writing in *Kettner's Book of the Table* published in 1877, describes what this brought about:

Below, there is a slow stewing going on; above, the meat is in a sort of miniature oven, baking and browning.

Today, braising pans often become detached from their lids, people believing the deep dish-shaped lid to be a totally separate utensil.

Right: Bain-marie

Far right: A patent bain-marie pot designed to fit into any saucepan containing hot water

The same fate is suffered by another French invention – the *bain-marie*. These once stood on the side of ranges in every middle- and upper-class kitchen. The *bain-marie* is reputed to have got its name from *bain*, meaning bath, and *marie*, a corruption of *mer* – the sea. It consisted of half a dozen or more lidded pots in various sizes, which stood in a shallow wide tin of warm water. The pots often rested on a trivet inside the bath. The *bain-marie* was admirably suited to making sauces, for they could be kept at a temperature equal to boiling water without actually boiling themselves. The attractive little pots were invariably made of copper and unfortunately it is rare now to find a *bain-marie* complete with all its pots as they are often sold off separately.

If the *bain-marie* was the gentlest method of using heat from the range, grilling was the fiercest. Before grilling could begin leaping flames had to be quenched by throwing a handful of salt on to them. Once the fire was 'clear' – that is, glowing red – a variety of gridirons could be placed over or in front of it. The bars of the gridiron had first to be rubbed with fat to stop the food sticking to them. The simplest type was like an iron frying pan with bars instead of a pan attached to the handle. More complex, were grills which hung in front of the fire, the food trapped between two rows of bars which had a small drip tray attached beneath. Some of these vertical grills were hinged so that food could be turned without removing the grill. Others were attached to a revolving spindle. Both types had modifications which allowed them to be slid up to, or away from, the heat.

A handy device for cooking small dishes such as a chop or sheep's heart was the American oven. This was an open-fronted metal box, its floor inclined to reflect heat. The article to be cooked was placed on a shelf halfway up the box and the box placed open front to the fire. Ruth once worked for a gentleman who insisted on his meat being roasted on an open fire. She used a bottle jack hung with worsted wool for joints and one of these small ovens for his rashers and chops. She used to stand the oven on a chair and push it up to the range. These small ovens worked on the same principle as the meat hastener, receiving and reflecting heat back from the range fire.

Many kitchens also had huge screens, which could be wheeled in front of the fire on castors. These screens had a multiplicity of purposes. On the side away from the fire they were flat and provided a welcome barrier between the kitchen staff and the heat of the range. On the side near the fire they were built like a cupboard with no door, the shelves of the cupboard being lined with shiny tin which reflected heat from the range. If a dish was cooked too soon, it could be placed on the tin-lined shelves to keep it warm until required. Similarly, before a meal was served, the plates to be used were polished and wrapped in paper by the second footman or hallboy and placed into the screen to warm. The screen was also a useful place to rest dishes whilst opening the oven door. Biscuits were stored at the top of the screen and firewood at the bottom to keep them dry. Some screens even had hinged doors which could be pushed back in order to get to the meat to baste it.

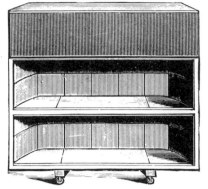

A roasting-screen, which doubled as a hot closet

To keep silver dishes warm it was usual to place them in a rack above the range. The kitchenmaids did this carefully, holding each dish in a cloth so that they did not leave their fingermarks on them. Fingermarks were sinful. Mrs May Bonning of Plymouth recalls that her first job as a kitchenmaid was to make gentleman's relish sandwiches. The plate she put the sandwiches on had a deep blue band around it. On taking the plate through the kitchen hatch, the butler noticed her fingermarks on the blue band and rearranged the sandwiches himself on a clean blue plate. Forever afterwards, she had to give her sandwiches to the butler on a white plate and he then transferred them to the dining-room china.

In 1838 Esther Copley's *Housekeeper's Guide* was saying:

There is nothing more awkward than to be obliged to put a joint or a pudding into too small a vessel for want of larger – or a small quantity of hash or gravy into a large saucepan for want of a smaller. It is poor economy that grudges a liberal supply of kitchen requisites...

Thirty years on, the postal service and printed catalogues were doing their best to ensure that no housewife should suffer such poor economy. William S. Burton of London, Furnishing Ironmonger by appointment to H.R.H. Prince of Wales, was sending post-free a catalogue listing every article needed to furnish a kitchen. The catalogue had 850 illustrations, plans of Mr Burton's twenty large show rooms and the reassuring information that the cost of delivering goods to the most distant parts of the United Kingdom by railway was 'trifling'.

A complete set of kitchen utensils suitable for a mansion was offered at £73 18s. 0d.; for a good class of house, £24 3s. 10d.; for a small house £10 12s. 5d., and for the smallest house, £3 19s. 0½d.

In answer to Mr Burton's and several other large ironmongers' hard sell, Mrs Jane Ellen Panton in her admirable book *From Kitchen to Garret* (in which the fictitious newly-wed couple Edwin and Angelina face and cope with domestic problems for the edification of real-life Victorian newly weds) warns that such set lists 'may generally be halved as regards the quantities with advantage...'. Even so, most kitchens needed an impressive number of stewpans, saucepans, fishkettles, sauté pans, steamers, boilers, sieves, colanders, moulds, funnels, dredgers and so on.

In well-to-do households, pans, bowls and moulds were generally made of copper with the initials of the owner of the house stamped prominently on to them, and, if the owner was titled, perhaps a coronet as well. Copper vessels ranged from ones so large that they could accommodate a haunch of venison down to moulds an inch or so in length used to steam delicate mixtures of pulversised white meat and cream. In the latter part of Victoria's reign, fashion and the availability of commercially made jelly mixes helped to swell the rows of copper by adding complex-shaped jelly moulds.

In Ruth's estimation copper pots are the most beautiful things to cook with. You could heat them easily, she says, and they lost heat just as quickly if you needed them to. They didn't wear out either – they were there when you started in a job and there when you left. But nothing is perfect and copper pots did have one drawback. Their insides had to be covered with a thin layer of tin. This was to prevent verdigris poisoning which could happen if food was left in contact with copper for any length

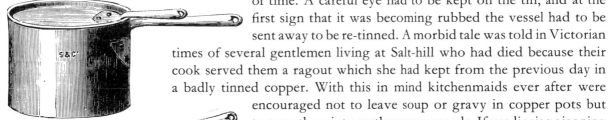

of time. A careful eye had to be kept on the tin, and at the first sign that it was becoming rubbed the vessel had to be sent away to be re-tinned. A morbid tale was told in Victorian times of several gentlemen living at Salt-hill who had died because their cook served them a ragout which she had kept from the previous day in a badly tinned copper. With this in mind kitchenmaids ever after were encouraged not to leave soup or gravy in copper pots but to pour them into earthenware vessels. If verdigris poisoning did occur, however, popular medical books advised the best antidote to be the whites of a dozen eggs beaten up in two pints of cold water, and a glassful taken every two minutes to encourage vomiting.

The first enamelled pots also presented a danger as they contained lead which could poison food left in them. Heavy and unglamorous as they were, iron saucepans seem to have been the safest – provided, that is, that they were dried carefully to prevent rust.

Almost as numerous as saucepans were strainers and sieves. Of the sieves there were ones made of black hair, others (more expensive) of white hair, ones with lawn or 'tammy' (a kind of woollen cloth) stretched

Round and oval stewpans made of copper

across them, and for coarser work, ones of cane or brass wire. Utensils like wooden mushrooms were used to force food through the sieves. You gripped the 'stem' and crushed with the 'mushroom' cap.

A set of scales was regarded as essential. Although expensive (a shopkeeper's account submitted in 1887 lists a set costing 19/9d.) they were worth their purchase for peace of mind. The cook could use them to check the weight of the meat delivered and to facilitate this operation the butcher was required to send a written note of the weight. If the scales corresponded with the note then all was well, but the note was kept to cross-check with the quarterly bill. Having a good set of scales also negated a kitchenmaid's excuse that 'the scales hadn't been working properly' when dishes she had prepared did not turn out successfully!

Sieving using a long-handled wooden spoon

Just as the need to heat food generated a whole range of kitchen devices, so too did the need to keep it cool. Ice had been used in preparing food as far back as 1667 when ice cream was served at a banquet at Windsor. At about the same time the French chef Vatel (who in 1671 killed himself in mortifcation when a turbot he'd ordered didn't arrive on time) had served Louis the Magnificent at Chantilly with fresh laid eggs in silver gilt cups. In fact, they weren't eggs at all – they were delicious ices made to look like eggs.

The ice needed to make desserts and to stop food deteriorating was stored in a variety of ways. Owners of parklands complete with handy lakes had their gardeners drag ice from the water in winter and store it in underground dome-shaped houses known as ice pits. Those unable to afford the luxury of a brick-built ice pit could store ice by making a snow stack. Ten-foot high hurdles were put round a piece of ground forty feet wide and a bed of brushwood faggots laid inside the hurdles. Snow was hauled onto this and, rather unhygienically, trampled underfoot by men and horses. Rock salt was thrown down to make each layer run into the next. Another row of hurdles was erected outside the first, and the gap between the two rows packed with stubble for insulation. With a thick covering of thatch, the stack could last as an ice source for the kitchen from June until October.

For those with neither ice pit nor snow stack, there were two options. They could buy it, either from the local fishmonger or direct from an importer (huge harvests of ice were made in Norway and America and shipped to this country for sale); or they could make it themselves, using complicated machines employing pumps, acid and dissolving salts. Most people opted for the convenient method of either sending a horse and cart

1

1 'The Victorian Kitchen Garden' at Chilton planted with nineteenth-century varieties of fruits and vegetables.

2 The garden in the productive days of late summer. Harry Dodson, head gardener, holds a basket filled with the first of the early apple crop.

2

4

*3 The kitchen before the
restoration work began.*

*4 The cream colour of the
dresser and cupboard was a
legacy of the last re-paint,
40 years ago.*

*5 Although rusted and broken,
to our delight the iron cooking
range still had the original
poker, flue scraper, and an old
cleaning brush.*

5

6 Ruth Mott. Ruth began her cooking career as a scullery maid in 1930. At that time mansion kitchens, complete with iron cooking ranges and hair sieves, were still run on Victorian lines. Remembering old kitchen practices Ruth felt brave enough to volunteer to be our 'Victorian Cook'.

7 Our first sight of the scullery, with its old, broken wooden plate rack.

8 The scullery refurbished and ready for use.

9 Ruth's kitchenmaid, Alison Arnison, more used to teaching music, takes down a vegetable tureen from the hot closet above the range.

10 Cleaning the range and making up the fire each morning was a task Alison's Victorian counterpart would have been only too familiar with.

11 The range in its cleaned and polished state and set with (left to right) tall stock pot, kettle and bain-marie.

12 A small selection of the copper utensils with which we filled the restored kitchen's walls and shelves.

13 The bain-marie, used during Victorian times to keep sauces warm.

14 Decorative jelly moulds.

11

12

13

14

15 *An open-fronted kitchen dresser filled with china and various copper moulds. At the right of the picture and fixed to the wall, the large, wooden pestle and mortar.*

16 *The cook's morning cup of tea placed on the dresser ready for delivery to her room.*

17 *Ruth demonstrates to Alison the heavy task of using the pestle and mortar.*

15

16

17

to the fishmonger or having him deliver half a hundred-weight once or twice a week – the frequency depending on the amount of entertaining being done.

Firms which sold ice also sold ice chests, the earliest forms of refrigerators. Described as 'handsome pieces of furniture', these wooden boxes held the ice block in the bottom and had sliding shelves in the upper part. Wines, fruits and provisions could be stored on separate shelves. Ice chests were suitable for the pantry.

Larger, more ornate refrigerators were used by the kitchen staff. When the block of ice arrived, it was wrapped either in clean sacking or a blanket and placed in a metal-lined cavity at the top of what looked for all the world like a sideboard. (Many such chests had elaborately curved backs and turned legs.) Articles to be kept especially cold could be stood on top of the sacking without fear of them slipping. Other food could be placed on perforated shelves in the cupboards beneath. Although the chest was well insulated, the block of ice would inevitably melt. To cope with this a channel was built into the design. It ran from the top cavity down to a brass tap at the bottom. To avoid sudden floods, kitchenmaids had to remember every so often to place a large basin under the tap, turn it on, and drain off as much water as they could.

The ability to store, if somewhat soggily, ice near the kitchen, helped create the fashion for serving ice cream and water ices at dinner. Despite some people's fears that ice cream forged together fat and gelatine in meat just consumed, causing chronic indigestion, it became the custom to eat ices as a last course.

A refrigerator or 'portable ice-chest'

Ice cream had to be made early in the day, especially if it was hot weather, so that it had time to freeze. Once the fruit had been pushed through a hair sieve, sugared and added to fresh cream, usually from the estate's dairy, the kitchenmaid had to break off a chunk from the big lump of ice in the top of the refrigerator. To do this she used a mallet and an ice-pricker (a device like a screwdriver with a pointed end). The ice then had to be crushed in the kitchen's tall pestle and mortar until all the pieces were of an even size. Once the ice was crushed, a freezing pail was brought. This was a bucket made of wood with a wooden bung near the base. Alternate layers of ice and coarse salt were then pressed into the bucket. Three pounds of ice combined with one pound of salt produced a temperature of -4 (minus four) degrees Fahreinheit. A cylindrical pewter ice pot was first plunged empty into the freezing mixture (this helped speed the eventual freezing process). When chilled it was removed and the ice cream put into it. Ice pots had tightly fitting lids with handles on top. Once a filled pot was plunged back into the freezing pail the kitchenmaid had to twist it in a semi-circular motion, first right, then left. Every ten minutes or so the action had to stop, the lid be taken off and an ice spatula inserted to cut away any frozen bits sticking to the sides. The spatula was like a small metal spade fitted to a long wooden handle. The frozen bits had to be carefully mixed with liquid in the centre and twisting resumed. If the ice had not been smashed into regular sized pieces in the initial preparation, the smaller bits would melt leaving only the bigger bits. If this happened the cream froze more slowly and unevenly.

Once the ice cream was stiff enough to stand a spoon in, it was ready for use. If a more elaborate shape was required, however, it could be transferred to a mould. Ice-cream moulds, made of pewter secured by clips, came in myriad designs from pineapples to baskets of flowers. It was prudent to chill them for half an hour before they were filled and then, so that all the nooks and crannies were properly packed, to fill the sides first before filling the middle. When this was done, the bung was taken out of the bottom of the ice pail and the melting water drained off. The pail was then topped up with fresh ice and salt and the mould plunged into it and left to freeze.

In addition to pewter moulds, there were conical or spherical ones called bombs. These were usually made of copper. Plain flat-topped bombs could be lined with thin paper before the ice cream was inserted – this helped the frozen ice cream slide out. A layer of greased paper was also put on top of the ice cream and sealed down with the lid. The joint between the lid and body of the bomb was heavily smeared with lard to stop any salt from the freezing bucket seeping into it.

Bomb moulds made it possible to combine two sorts of ice in one. If a thin coating of fruit water ice (frozen fruit juice sweetened with syrup) was put into the mould before the ice cream was packed in, when the mould was turned out the ice cream would have a film of coloured ice over it. Alternatively, the bomb could be taken out of the freezing pail after four or five hours, a hole scooped out of the middle of the ice cream, a filling of fresh fruit or pieces of chocolate inserted and the bomb returned to the pail to continue freezing.

Invariably bomb moulds stood either on a stem base which unscrewed, or had a knob on the top that unscrewed. When the ice cream had to be turned out the kitchenmaid took out the screw, put a small piece of muslin over the screw-hole and, placing her lips against the muslin, blew gently into the hole. The heat of her breath was sufficient to separate the ice cream from the sides of the mould and make it slip onto a waiting dish. Once on the dish, if it was a really bombshell-shaped ice cream, the battle-

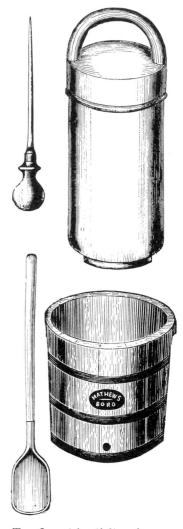

Top: Ice pricker (left) and freezing pot
Above: Ice spatula and ice pail

Below: Bomb moulds

PULSOMETER ENGINEERING C° L?

PE C? L?

THE "CHAMPION" HAND ICE MACHINE

IS THE

SIMPLEST AND MOST RELIABLE

IN THE MARKET.

INVALUABLE IN HOT CLIMATES.

No expensive Freezing Powders or Ice Chest required.

THE MACHINE IS ALWAYS READY FOR USE.

Will Ice Water and Wines for the Table in Three minutes. Will Cool Butter, make Ice Creams and Block Ice, &c.

No. 1 size (as shown), suitable for Yachts, Shooting Parties, and small Families, &c., £8 8s. Attachment for Icing Bottled Wines, &c., 10s. extra. Ice Cream Jar, 5s. extra.

No. 2 size, most suitable for Domestic use and Export, £12. Extras as above. Packing in all cases extra.

No. 3 size, to make from 4 to 5 lbs. ice per hour, £20.

No. 5 size can be worked by Hand or Strap, will make from 15 to 25 lbs. of Block Ice per hour, or about 100 lbs. per day. Price £75.

Send for Illustrated List No. F6, post free.

PURE ICE

AT A MOMENTS NOTICE.

MANY HUNDREDS ARE BEING SOLD.

9 ELMS IRON WORKS, LONDON, S.W.

An advertisement from the journal The Ironmonger, *August, 1890*

like illusion was often enhanced by adding spun barley sugar to its centre so that it looked like a flaming shell about to explode!

There were other fancy ice dishes like soufflés which, because they were not totally enclosed in moulds, could not be plunged in an ice bucket. To freeze these an ice cave was used. This was a round or square box into which the dish was placed. The cave was then buried upright in freezing mixture.

Ruth recalls the slightly bizarre task of making ice cream in a saucepan. She made it in a saucepan because she only had to make a little bit. Her gentleman employer liked blackcurrant ice cream for his tea every day. She put ice and freezing salt into a bowl and swung the saucepan by its handle backwards and forwards through the ice.

The drudgery of making large amounts of ice cream by hand was alleviated by an American invention – the ice cream making machine.

This was an ice bucket with a pot inside. The pot fitted into a socket at the bottom of the bucket and into a socket attached to a rotary arm at the top. The usual mixture of salt and ice was then rammed between the outside of the pot and the insides of the bucket. When the handle was turned it turned the pot. To speed up the process some machines had a double action, with the pot and stirrer turning in opposite directions.

Patent ice-cream freezer

The ice-cream machine was one labour-saving device that did find its way into large kitchens. On the whole, however, where labour was plentiful culinary operations continued to be done by hand. Even as late as the 1930s some women suffered aching arms from having to beat every egg with only their hand for 20 minutes, or had their finger nails ground down by sugar as they hand-mixed cakes.

Smaller Victorian kitchens where a cook-general worked, sometimes helped by the mistress, were probably the places most likely to invest in the many culinary gadgets which came mostly from America (where there was a servant shortage).

The Archimedian egg whisk (a rotary whisk) was invented in 1861. It retailed at one shilling, and the makers boasted that it could do double the work of the old wire whisks with half the effort. The Novel Egg Boiler had a whistle attached to the boiler which, activated by the rising steam, blew when the eggs were done. There were also meat mincers, sausage machines, apple parers, potato parers, cucumber slicers, radish scrapers and even a pea sheller. The makers of the pea sheller claimed it could shell a peck of peas in ten minutes.

Stanley's Patent Heat Conductors were intriguing. These objects looked like skewers and were sold under the guise of 'Scientific Cookery'. For 2s. 9d. they apparently saved time, firing and one pound of meat in every ten. One had to send for them to find out how they worked. Perhaps Arthur Line, Inventor of Chislehurst, had the neatest invention of all – announced to the world in 1887, his two-lipped saucepan enabled you to pour with the left hand and stir with the right.

CHAPTER FIVE

Victorian Values

Cleanliness is the most essential ingredient in the art of cooking: a dirty kitchen being a disgrace to mistress and maid.

Fat Housekeepers make Lean Executors.

nne Cobbett fought back the exclamation, 'Dirty pigs!' and thought of England. Sympathetic to an ailing fellow traveller she had descended to the kitchens of a French hotel to instruct the chef in the English art of making beef tea. She found black walls, black utensils ('of what their insides might be I did not ascertain'), and a kitchen table strewn with fragments of fish, fowl and pastry and which rivalled the walls for blackness. There was also a wild-looking fire with a matching chef. Up to that point she had been quite enjoying her stay but, as she told her readers in *The English Housekeeper*:

I never recovered the feeling of perfect security in what I was about to eat until the sea again rolled between me and the kitchen of the Hôtel de l'Europe, and I again actually saw the dear bright fire, the whitened hearth, the yellow-ochre walls, the polished tins, the clean-scrubbed tables and chairs, and the white dresser cloths, of my kitchen.

The maxim that dirt might be hated but that it should never be hidden was vigorously upheld in the Victorian kitchen. Floors, tables, workboards, passages and shelves were forever being scrubbed down. Scrubbing was

Alison, doing her best to scrub the kitchen table clean

part of the workload of the scullery maid and second kitchenmaid. First thing in the morning, covered in big, hard aprons and armed with hot water laced with crushed soda, Calais sand and a hard scrubbing brush, they tackled the wooden table-tops. Soap was not used lest it remain on the table and the taste came off onto the foods. First the table was wet then the sand sprinkled over it and scrubbed well. The table legs had to be wiped down too and then the whole table rinsed with ice-cold water to make the wood 'set'. Many kitchens had blocks of stone under the legs of wooden furniture to prevent water collecting under them and rotting the wood – a necessary precaution for floors, like tables, could be scrubbed as many as three times a day.

Soft soap could be used on floors. It was made of whale or train oil mixed with potash and, although more expensive than ordinary soap, you didn't have to use as much. It was hard on the hands; the caustic potash bit into cuticles and left skin cracked and tender. Some kitchen floors had stone flags while others had some sort of covering – but they all got the same scrubbing down. There were several types of floor covering in use at the time. Oil cloth was mostly laid in small kitchens and water often got between it and the floor beneath, rotting the floor. Eventually the paint would also come off the oil cloth. The best floor covering was linoleum. Running it a close second was Parkesine, a rubbery substance made from an Indian shrub. (This material was also used for covering submarine cables.) Once Parkesine was rolled out flat it could be painted like oil cloth. In some kitchens sawdust was scattered over the floor after it had been cleaned. This helped to catch and contain any particles of food which accidentally dropped. The sawdust was swept up in the afternoon before the floor was scrubbed again.

The cook oversaw and inspected cleaned floors and shelves. She could use the exercise as a platform for tyranny. Mrs Margaret Pettit of Ousden near Newmarket told me that when she was 14 the cook she worked under used to make her scrub and then polish the kitchen floor before she was allowed to go out for her half-day off; and as she said, anybody knows you can't get a shine on a wet floor. Ruth remembers having to scrub out the shelves and floor of a larder every morning and says that if the cook didn't like what she saw when she came to inspect it she used to take all the vegetables off the shelves and throw them into the middle of the floor. After she'd stomped off Ruth had to pick everything up and start all over again. It can't have been that Ruth wasn't trying. She spent so long kneeling and scrubbing that her knees used to wear through her black stockings and she was always having to reinforce them. She found the best way to do this was to cut out the middle of the leg between the knee and the ankle of the last pair. This made a big patch for the front of the

Alison in the scullery, putting to use a pulley-operated drying line

most recently holed pair. The cook also made her reinforce the floor cloths by sewing the sides to the middle to make them last longer.

Of other cloths, pudding cloths and jelly bags had to be washed directly after use or soaked in cold water until they could be washed. After washing they were thoroughly dried and stored away from dust.

Dustbins were often banned from the kitchen or scullery, mistresses believing that they encouraged waste. All organic refuse had to be burnt by throwing in onto the fire grate and covering it with hot ashes, or in big houses, tipped down stone chutes into pig bins. Dustbins were also bad because they could cause the kitchen to smell. Smells in small houses were not 'nice'. Mrs Panton, in *From Kitchen to Garret*, outlines the problem in her own inimitable style:

I cannot tell how it is, but a domestic appears to me to be born into the world bereft of any sense of smell. They never can smell anything. You will go into the kitchen and discover an odour enough to appal you and you will say, 'What is this terrible smell, I wonder', but your cook will reply 'Smell, Mum? Oh I don't smell anything, perhaps it have drifted in at the window'. But do not be daunted by that. Do not for one moment think you are wrong and she is right, but persevere, and hunt that smell down, and ten chances to one you will find something that requires your immediate attention in the sink line . . .

Disinfectant was the obvious remedy and copious amounts of Condy's fluid disappeared down drain holes. This was a disinfectant described as 'efficacious but unobjectionable'. There were two kinds, red and green. The red was sometimes prescribed by doctors as safe to drink, the green was cheaper and best for drains. An effective disinfectant could be made by diluting one teaspoonful of Condy's in one pint of water. One wineglass full of Condy's (a halfpenny's worth) made a gallon of disinfectant.

A useful way of stopping drains from becoming clogged by fatty pans was to put a lump, say half a pound, of soda over the drain hole. Renewed every couple of days, this acted as a percolator and cut the grease content in the used water.

Grease also sank into the sides of wooden washing-up bowls and was difficult to remove. For this reason, although wood helped prevent chipping, many people preferred tin washing-up bowls. The best china was washed by the housekeeper, but all the kitchen pots, pans, cooking utensils and servants' crockery were done by the scullery maid. She used hot water from the boiler at the side of the range or water heated in a copper in the scullery.

Ruth says that she finds that no one today knows how to wash up. Instructing her seconded scullery/kitchenmaid Alison, she laid down the principles: sort things out according to size before you start, because it saves time later – big plates at the bottom, next size on top and so on –

The nearer the plate rack, the easier the task

for if everything is done in size it goes into the drying rack easily; plates must always be put into the rack and never wiped dry as this leaves them looking greasy. Alison was using a 'new' plate rack, for when we'd discovered our Victorian kitchen the large old plate rack on the teak draining board had been in a very bad condition. The bottom row of rungs, in particular, had been so decrepit, that the whole rack had to be re-made. Ruth knew why the bottom rungs had gone. It was simply, she said, that most scullery maids had been so small that to avoid soggy armpits when racking-up they always used the lower row!

Alison got one bowl of hot water for washing and one bowl of cold for rinsing. Ruth showed her how to use soft soap and soda whisked together in the hot water.

Victorian instruction books confirmed Ruth's method and gave additional tips: the water in which plates and dishes were washed should be put aside for pigs; a handful of bran in the water produces a fine polish on crockeryware; use soda and hot water to wash tea things; tea stains inside the cups can be removed with a bit of salt. An additional instruction was that (like the wooden table tops) rolling pins, paste boards and chopping boards must not be washed with soap, because of it 'tasting', but should be rubbed with Calais sand and hot water, then rinsed in cold. The amount of Calais sand used for cleaning appears to have been enormous.

As even a warm finger, accidentally placed upon it, could mark a glass, all good glassware was cleaned in the butler's pantry by the footmen or hallboy. Knives, if not cleaned by the undergardener, were also seen to in the butler's pantry. Because hot water would discolour ivory and loosen

Victorian table knives in various styles

Rotary knife-cleaner

the handles, only the knife blades were placed in it. The handles were washed separately in warm water and a little salt used to clean off any stains. The most generally used method of keeping the blades bright (bearing in mind that at that time knife blades stained as soon as put in water) was to rub them on a knife board which had been covered with brick dust, which had to be carefully dusted off the handles before they were put away. Rubbing knife blades on a board wrapped in a piece of carpet also gave them a high polish. Knives which were being put away for some time had their blades rubbed over with mutton suet to keep them from rusting. Rotary knife-cleaning machines, which were wooden cylinders filled with sand and brushes into which knives were inserted in slots, could clean up to a dozen knives at a time. But these had to be used with care for if the knives were pushed in too far, the machine wore out the shoulders and blunted the edges of the blades.

Back in the scullery washing sieves could cause problems. Raw chicken and fish were often pushed through hair sieves to make garnishes. If a scullery maid washed the sieve afterwards in hot water, any remaining bits of flesh cooked and it was practically impossible to get the thing clean. Anxious kitchenmaids responsible for using these sieves tried to make sure that the scullery maid remembered to use cold water. If she wasn't worrying about sieves or trying to keep awake, the scullery maid had greasy spits, gridirons, dripping pans and tin and iron frying pans to clean with hot water, soda and, of course, Calais sand. Tin was also cleaned with a mixture of rotten stone (crushed, weathered limestone) and rape oil which was washed off with boiling water. All utensils had to be wiped out and stood near the range to dry and so prevent rusting.

New vessels had to be cleaned before use, too. A live coal was popped inside a tin saucepan and shaken up and down to get rid of the resin taste of new tin. It was also recommended that two tablespoons of bran be boiled in water in any new saucepan, and then simmered for two hours to make the inside smooth enough to use.

Kettles kept on the range had to have the soot scraped off the sides regularly for soot, being a bad conductor of heat, would slow down boiling time.

But of all the vessels in the kitchen, the most public and apparent testimony to the cleanliness of the cook and her kitchen were her coppers. These were the pots, pans and moulds made of copper lined with a thin coat of tin. In some kitchens there could be as many as 300 pieces of copper and all were displayed – for, as the *Housekeeper's Guide* had said in 1838, 'They will not be placed out of sight, but every copper, stewpan and saucepan will be kept bright without and well tinned and clean within.' If these coppers were the gleam in the cook's eye, they filled the

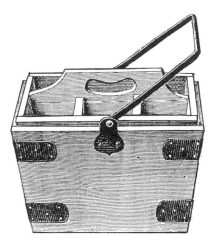

Above: A late Victorian advertisement for cleaning brushes (left) and a housemaid's box for cleaning materials

kitchenmaid's soul with a shadow as gloomy as the tarnish the coppers frequently took on when the weather was damp and foggy. Women who had worked with such cooks and their coppers told me, 'We always prayed that the cook wouldn't use too many copper pans because they all had to be cleaned', and 'There was an incessant cleaning of copper, you'd never dare put them away tarnished.' Mrs Hardy, the cook at Chirk Castle, used to take prospective kitchenmaids into her kitchen to show them all the gleaming copper pans. She always said, 'You see all those copper pans along there?' Meek reply: 'Yes, ma'am.' 'Well, I want my coppers looking exactly like that, like a new penny, every one of them, big or small, and the inside must look like a silver threepenny bit. Can you do that?' Even meeker reply: 'Yes, ma'am.' 'Right.'

The method of cleaning coppers varied. Mrs Crosby told me that she hadn't been in the job very long when one day she was told to be up at 4 o'clock the following morning in order to clean all the copperware. She and another kitchenmaid worked with two gallons of brewers yeast in a big brown jug and a bucket of silver sand. With a mixture of the yeast and sand they had to scour each copper with their bare hands, then rinse it in clear water and drain it. The more coppers they cleaned, the more they began to get drunk and merry from the smell of the yeast – so much so that by breakfast time, helped by empty stomachs, they were both roaring and laughing uncontrollably – but the coppers had a lovely shine.

There were less hilarious methods of burnishing copper. Some people used silver sand and ginger, others salt, vinegar and sand. The most common was a mixture of silver sand and soft soap for the copper on the outside of the vessel, and a paste made of flour, sand, soft soap and lemon for the silver-tinned inside. Ruth told Alison to keep all her old lemon rinds and use them to rub the sand into the nooks and crannies of the jelly moulds, adding that the sand would wear her fingernails down so much that she'd never need to file them again. The big round copper egg bowls did not have silver-tinned interiors and Alison always cleaned these with lemon and salt before they were used.

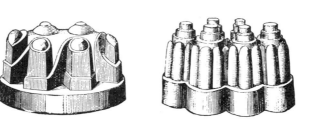

Decorative copper moulds

It is not surprising that in winter especially, the daily application of sand, various acids, soda and soft soap, left kitchen and scullery maids with chapped and bleeding hands. Catherine M. Buckton, in *Food and Home Cookery* published in 1879, was advising girls to buy a small bottle of glycerine directly their hands began to chap, and rub some of it over their hands followed by flour before going to bed. Glycerine was obtained from the manufacture of soap and, mixed with elderflower water, it was also used to protect complexions from cutting winds and frost. As an interesting digression, ladies also treated their hands at night but having more time their cosmetic ritual was more elaborate. They minced separately, wax, spermaceti, white soap, and mutton suet, and melted these over a water bath. They then added olive oil, pomade rosat, benzoin, Peru balsam, essence of roses and honeywater and stirred these and the soap mixture together until melted. Taking a brush, they then applied the mixture to the wrong side of a pair of gloves, turned the gloves back to the right way, blew them up and put them in a warm place to dry. If worn every night the pair of gloves would last a fortnight. There is a similarity between this recipe and the one Ruth used – well, a small similarity, namely the use of gloves. By Ruth's day kitchenmaids had a choice of a natural method (mutton fat) or a product called 'Snowfire'. Ruth bought 'Snowfire', which stung when it was rubbed in. She washed her hands in hot water every night, rubbed on the green, pungent mixture, then put on a pair of gloves so that it would soak in and the bedsheets wouldn't get greasy. In the morning, as Ruth said, her hands were nice and soft and quite ready to start off the washing-up all over again.

Victorian jewellers always had their lamps *outside* their shop windows because gas tarnished silver and the more impure the gas the worse the tarnish. Similarly, gas lights in dining rooms tarnished silver serving plates and dishes. In large houses this was the butler's problem and cleaning was dealt with in his pantry by footmen. In small houses serving dishes and covers were more likely to be made of the increasingly available electro-plated nickel silver. With no butler, it would fall to the kitchen staff to clean these. The methods were various. After washing, the dishes might simply be rubbed over with a piece of flannel soaked in salad oil and then polished with a soft cloth. Alternatively, whitening might be moistened with whisky, rubbed on, then brushed off with a soft plate brush and the dishes polished with a dry washing leather.

In small houses where there weren't many housemaids, the kitchen might also be called on to provide cleaning help upstairs. The kitchen-cum-scullery maid might perhaps have to clean the cook/housekeeper's room first thing in the morning. For this she would have to keep all her tea leaves, squeeze them out as dry as possible (as tea leaves could stain) and sweep them across the room carpet towards the fireplace before brushing them up and starting the fire.

'Elbow grease'

There were some awful houses where alas, the kitchen staff (of one) did everything upstairs and more besides too. Below is part of a schedule drawn up for a maid-of-all-work. This excerpt is for Saturday alone:

Light the kitchen fire, open the house, clean the boots, take them up with the hot water. Do the dining-room fire-side, sweep up the pieces, dust, lay the breakfast; dust the drawing room, clean the fan-light and glass door, thoroughly clean the passage, sweep and rub the walls, beat the mats, clean the steps, clean the kitchen stairs.

Strip the beds, empty the slops, fill the jugs and bottles, take away the breakfast, wash up. Make the beds, dust the rooms and the stairs, clean the knives and chamber candlesticks. Thoroughly clean the kitchen, scullery, and all below. Attend to the meals; wash up.

Go to bed at   o'clock.

The blank for when she went to bed was presumably left for the maid-of-all-work to fill in; providing that she had the energy. Sunday and every other day of the week were of much the same pattern, perhaps the major room to be cleaned differing each day. It was recommended that the mistress write the weekly work schedule in plain large letters so that the maid could have no excuse that she hadn't done it all because she couldn't read everything!

If cleanliness was next to godliness in the Victorian household, then waste was the work of the devil – waste was sinful. Many Victorian domestic economists preached that France held a lesson for the British kitchen. In that country, they said, nothing was wasted, cooks both private and public made excellent easily digestible food out of substances that the British would throw away. French railway stations always had good cheap, nourishing soup and the French army fed itself on the rudest of nature's gifts while the English army, despite appliances and supplies, was half-starved.

There were even such dire warnings as: 'It is much feared, that for the waste of many of the good things that God has given for our use, no abuse, the mistress and servants of great houses will hereafter be called to a strict account.' This was unfair for as the French had their pot au feu into which scraps went, the Victorian kitchen had its 'digester' and its stockpot.

The digester, used more in small kitchens than large, was an iron pot with a lid which had a valve in the centre. The lid was firmly secured by twisting it beneath three bits of metal soldered to the rim of the pot. Bones and water could be put into a digester and with the lid in place, heat would make the pressure within the pot rise sufficiently to make the bones give out all their gelatine. These early pressure cookers gained a reputation for being the most economical of all cooking utensils and were viewed as indispensable in small kitchens, where if one was lucky enough to have a 'thoughtful' cook, no bone, even a fish bone, was thrown away but converted into stock and the basis of soups.

As indispensable in big households were stockpots. These tall saucepans with well-fitting lids outlived digesters in private kitchens. Ruth said of them: 'You can't really work a kitchen without a stockpot, all the old cooks and chefs set great store by them – they were the things that formed the basis of most of the work.' It was the same tale from all women of Ruth's background and generation, with one lady joking that just about everything except his lordship's socks went into the stockpot.

Stockpot

Big kitchens always had two stockpots, a white one for white soup and a brown one for brown soup. The white one was 'started off' by putting veal and chicken carcasses into it and the brown one with roast beef bones. Using roast bones cut down on the fat and beef was better than lamb because lamb was too fatty. Oddments of lean meat, chopped carrot and an onion were then added. Ruth preferred the onion skin to be left on, for that, like roastng the bones first, gave the stock a good colour. You had to be careful she said about putting too much vegetable in because it made the stock ferment and any soup made from it would be cloudy. The pots simmered on the range all day until 9 o'clock at night when they were strained off through a hair sieve. Next day the pots went back on to simmer again and collect more scraps. If the stock that was strained off was rich enough it was boiled down to make glaze. The Victorian *Manual of Domestic Economy* estimated that a quart of stock made about an inch to an inch and a half of glaze. The *Manual of Domestic Economy* also thought that it was much less trouble and cost to buy glaze, but even by Ruth's day this advice wasn't followed. (In fact it was turned on its head – the cooks Ruth worked under sold glaze to shops, with both Fortnum and Masons and Jacksons paying well for it.) When the glaze cooled it hardened and it was put into skins like sausages. The sausage strips were hung up and bits cut off to either simmer in a pot in the *bain-marie* so that glaze was always to hand or to have water added to make gravy or sauce. If a family owned a country house in Scotland the kitchen staff were able to make great quantities of venison glaze during their vacation. The glaze was carried back and stored in tins so that it would last.

Before Ruth's day, the economic value of the stockpot was furthered by the practice of using fat (taken off the cooled stock) for cakes and pastries. The fat was clarified by putting it into the oven until it melted then pouring it off into a clean jar. Water and any particles of meat fell to the bottom of the jar, leaving clean fat at the top. Ruth made dripping (the cook's perk) in the same way, emptying the meat tin and dripping tray with the cook standing over her to make sure that she got out every last drop. She boiled the fat until it was hot and then put boiling water into it and stood it to one side until it hardened. Once solid she cut it into sections and turning the pieces upside down scraped the bits off the bottom. The whole procedure than had to be gone through again until the dripping was absolutely pure.

Ruth says she never encountered waste in the kitchens she worked in and another retired kitchenmaid said that one thing working in service taught you was thrift. She remembers all crusts and stale bread being put into a tin and browned in the oven to make breadcrumbs. Potato peelings brought disgrace to another kitchenmaid, who was reported by the man who collected the pigswill bucket for peeling them too thick. Mushroom skins were kept to fill omelettes or flavour egg on toast and even peashells were sorted over and the best carefully browned in a cool oven. They were used to flavour soups and give them a golden colour. Most Victorians would have agreed with the Reverend Faunthorpe, who wrote in *Household Science* in 1881 that waste was abominable ingratitude to God not to mention knavish dishonesty to the master and mistress.

The economic running of her kitchen was a trial to a Victorian wife of the middle classes. She was totally dependent upon her husband for money, but taught that she mustn't worry him with domestic details. Without ever having managed money or a kitchen before, it's little wonder that some girls were charged with reducing their husband to a 'recurring vicissitude of one day's feasting and three or four days' fasting, with an intermediate day of scraps.' Towards the latter end of the nineteenth century, a fall in food prices made budgeting easier. With imports from New Zealand, the price of meat was over halved, fish and game were less expensive than they had been during the middle of the century and tinning made salmon no longer a luxury. Sugar also fell from 6d. to 2d. a pound and a loaf of bread was $5\frac{1}{2}$d. instead of 9d.

Despite this, one housewife calculating the economy of her kitchen made an alarming discovery – the price of a leg of mutton was three guineas. It might have started off from the butcher's at $7\frac{1}{2}$d, but by the time she'd taken into account the high rent of her house, with its extra rooms to accommodate the cook and kitchenmaid who cooked the leg and the footman who served it, the combined wages of the servants and the price of the fuel on which the leg was cooked, it ended up costing three guineas. Augusta Webster proclaimed her discovery in a paper entitled 'A Housewife's Opinion' and at the same time voiced the fears of many, that instead of getting a good return for their housekeeping allowance, husbands were paying out to keep an establishment of servants. Mrs Webster had a novel solution. She believed that as a lot of people were warmed by the earth's one sun, so a lot of people's food could be cooked by one fire. Writing at the time of a building boom when, as Mrs Webster put it, houses were being 'thrown up' and when 'daughters wooed by the help of express trains would scarcely feel themselves married at all unless transplanted', Mrs Webster knocked on the head the idea of the sanctity of home and hearth. Instead she proposed home-hotels which would give the privacy of home but the freedom from household cares that hotels gave. Inmates would order meals, pay for them and eat them at moderate prices occasioned by the economy of mass catering on, as she said, a large, wholesome scale.

Mrs Webster wasn't sufficiently dazzled by her own idea that she didn't see the odd drawback. For example a woman inmate might offer a visitor a cup of tea but at the same time shudder with a presentiment of despair, 'foreseeing that her friend will have gone home to dinner long before the operation of getting it will have been concluded.' Despite such drawbacks the scheme of a co-operative home would, Mrs Webster believed, transmute well into the blocks of 'flats' then being built. The flats unfortunately had the appearance of factories, but with mass catering they could be, she was sure, factories of domestic bliss.

CHAPTER SIX
The Kitchen and the Garden

Vegetables are at their best when just on the eve of being ripe,
in their natural season....

dwin Beckett, head gardener to Lord Aldenham at Elstree in Hertfordshire, really knew how to grow vegetables. In late Victorian times Mr Beckett set a record by winning for Lord Aldenham (for it was the master who always got the credit, not the gardener) ten gold medals for vast and beautiful vegetable exhibits. The only man I know of ever to equal that achievement is my friend Harry Dodson. Harry re-created, becoming famous in the process, *The Victorian Kitchen Garden.* To do this he drew on over forty years' experience as a head gardener and during twelve of those years he too, won ten gold medals for his employer. The similarity between Harry and his Victorian counterpart doesn't end there. Mr Beckett made the perspicacious remark: 'High quality is the standard of judgment, size alone counts for little on the exhibition table, and has few friends in the kitchen.' Judging vegetables for the Royal Horticultural Society, Harry knows about quality as opposed to size; and having supplied produce to cooks in mansion kitchens since boyhood, he also knows that they preferred the youngest, smallest and tenderest vegetables.

Harry, slightly more blunt than Mr Beckett, called such culinary pre-dilection, murder of a crop. He said, 'You'd have something coming along and there was potential for a wonderful crop which was going to reach perfection and hardly before it began to turn in you had to pull it to pieces and send it to the kitchen.' He agreed that young vegetables were no doubt a great delicacy but it was a real problem for gardeners to keep up the supply to the mansion when the material the kitchen wanted was always so small.

When it was considered vulgar to eat vegetables, Beau Brummell admitted that he believed he had once eaten a pea. Consumption of peas had gone up considerably by Victorian times – in fact vegetable connoisseurs of that age were calling the pea 'The Prince of the Vegetable Garden' and horticulturists were making great strides to improve its early cropping, succulence and sweetness. When he wasn't about his duties as MP for Monmouthshire (1841 to 1847), antiquarian and gourmet Octavius

Harry holding a choice display of vegetables from the kitchen garden

Morgan made a hobby of collecting recipes and food tips. Many he wrote on the notepaper of the houses he was staying in at the time or on fragments of blue paper from the Athenaeum Club, where probably he was pleased to collect from a certain Colonel Woodward the following. He marked it 'For Peas at Christmas':

McLean's 'Little Gem' to be sown in pots in September and October to be placed under a north wall so that the pots may become filled with roots and then put into a warm House.

Pea-shelling machine. It shelled with 'extraordinary rapidity'

The 'House' in question was a glasshouse. Harry knows all about forcing peas – many's the batch of pots he's put into warm vineries and peach houses. Doctor Kitchiner (another Victorian gourmet) estimated that a cook should allow a peck of peas to two hearty pea eaters (one peck being equivalent to two pints – one litre). This amount was trimmed in later cookery books to a peck of young peas to 6 to 8 persons. Even when it was warm enough to grow them in the main vegetable plots of the kitchen garden, peas still had to be picked when very small. It was, said Harry, a proper headache because of course you needed so many to get the right amount.

The Journal of Horticulture (understandably on the side of the gardener) put the final responsibility firmly on the kitchen staff. In an 1871 edition it was stated that, as it was impossible for any gardener to be quite sure that every pea was of the same age, care should be bestowed in the kitchen whilst shelling. If one pea was found to be older than the rest it should be left out, for that one pea would spoil the whole dish.

Broad beans, often simply referred to in the past as the garden bean, had also to be tediously small. Ruth recalls having to peel the skin off each broad bean twice if a batch arrived in the kitchen slightly bigger than standards of perfection allowed. This made the beans just about acceptable, for broad beans suffered from old prejudices which labelled them as more or less 'objectionable' articles of diet. They were, it was said, indigestible, heating, oppressive to the stomach, gave little nourishment and – worst of all – productive in flatulence.

Broad beans

The servants' hall coped with what the dining room could not, for the niceties of midget vegetables extended only to the master's table. When broad beans were brought in with black eyes in them Ruth knew they were for the servants' meals. It was the same with carrots. The family was served tiny, tender carrots. These had been carefully forced out-of-season on hotbeds of fermenting material made up under garden frames. The servants, meanwhile, ate last season's big old carrots which were stacked under sand and kept in the garden's vegetable store.

When Harry was a young journeyman (the name given to garden

apprentices), it was his responsibility to go each morning to collect the cook's order. She would have an idea of what was available in the garden, for the head gardener would have sent word of what was ready and what he recommended. The head gardener tried not to let her know of anything that, if he picked it, was still so young that there was nothing to follow it up. Cooks were renowned for having a 'run' for a couple of days on anything young and choice. This mild subterfuge was occasionally shot to pieces if the master and his family, inspecting the kitchen garden after church on a Sunday morning, spotted an under-age delicacy and specially requested it of the cook in the following week.

Harry stood in awe of the cook. He knew she was an important part of estate life. She was close to the lady of the house and had to please her. If anything went wrong and the cook got the blame she could, if she thought it appropriate, shift the blame to the head gardener. The blame then went all down the line from the head gardener to the man in charge of fruit-under-glass, to the kitchen garden foreman and finally to Harry, the young journeyman, who would be blamed for not taking things up to the house as they should have been.

Harry used to take the cook's order back to the kitchen garden foreman and between them they got together whatever vegetables she wanted. The more exotic fruits – melons, pineapples, apricots, peaches and the huge dessert red and yellow gooseberries – were picked later in the day, often by the head gardener, and went not to the kitchen but directly to the butler or housekeeper. Harry recalls that when he was a very small boy his uncle, who was head gardener to the Earl of Selborne, used to send him to the kitchen in the afternoon with fruit for the desserts to be made the following day. Victorian scientific thinking held that fruit, if not gathered until the afternoon, had had the benefit of the day's light and heat upon it, necessary to convert acid to sugar and make it far sweeter tasting than if picked in the morning.

Not needing such sweetness, vegetables had to be in the kitchen each morning and Harry carried them there in two deep baskets capable of holding a bushel apiece and suspended from a yoke across his shoulders. He generally saw no one, but unloaded the vegetables into their appropriate slats in the vegetable store. A large shallow bowl containing half an inch of water was on a slab by the slats – into this he put the small French beans which were tied with bass into little bundles and bulkier, but equally neat, bundles of asparagus. Both of these vegetables came under the heading 'choice'. French beans were the only vegetables which, in forcing, shared the rarefied heat of pineapple pits. Any other winter lodger might infest that precious fruit crop with bugs. In addition to improving peas, Victorian seedsmen took French beans to new heights –

quite literally, for they bred an entirely new race, one that climbed. These are not to be confused with runner beans which at that time were known as scarlet runners, and which were originally grown solely for the beauty of their flowers. It was not until the end of the eighteenth century that a gardener discovered that the flower seed-pods were good to eat.

A basket of freshly picked beans

Some old gardening books talk about French beans and others about kidney beans. It seems that the bigger a French bean was, the more likely it was to be called a kidney bean. If all this is a bit confusing, so too is contemporary advice on preparing the beans. Eliza Acton, in her *Modern Cookery* written in 1855, says if the beans are small, they should merely be topped and tailed before boiling; but when they are from half to two parts grown, they should be cut obliquely into a lozenge form or, 'when a less modern fashion is preferred, split them lengthwise into delicate strips and then cut them once across'. Ten years later *The Complete Cookery-Book* agreed about sending them up whole if small but said that if they were older they should be cut across in a *slanting* direction, and for the common table, split and divided across. By 1890, *The Encyclopaedia of Practical Cookery* recommended cutting them slantingly, not in shreds, or they would lose their flavour; if they were being used for garnishing, they should be cut into diamond shapes.

So what was the standard Victorian way of preparing French beans? Ruth plumped for the lengthways and one cut across method. It was what she'd done years ago, especially for garnishing. She used to cut about twelve beans like this, and then tie them up in little bunches and put them around a saddle of lamb. Alison got into difficulties – her strips were less than straight, particularly if a bean seed disobligingly got into the pathway of her descending blade. A case of practice makes perfect or, as Ruth said, 'By the time you've done 3 or 4 bushels, Alison, you'll have got the hang of it.'

How to cut beans into diamonds for garnishing (left) and lengthways cut for boiling

There was no such confusion over preparing asparagus. Harry had always been taught to put asparagus for the kitchen into bundles of 25 sticks, and instructions in an 1850 receipt confirmed this was the amount then recommended – with three such bundles being sufficient for a medium-sized dish.

Asparagus

When Harry first came to Chilton as a head gardener there was a quarter of an acre laid down to this vegetable. Growing asparagus meant a lot of work but he knew the house set great store on the tender green sticks. Each morning the beds were gone over and the best cut and bundled. Each 25 sticks had to be of equal size in their respective bundles. The bundles were either placed in very wet sand or in shallow water and would be collected in this way for two or three days before being taken up to the mansion or sent away to the family's London house. Thin, rangey, sticks were known as sprue. Many old cooks liked the gardener to bring sprue to the kitchen so that they could make asparagus 'peas' when real peas were not in season. The 'peas' were bits broken off the sprue top into pieces the size of peas. These were then bottled and served with either white sauce or melted butter.

Harry's garden now had nothing like its former quarter of an acre of asparagus beds – in fact, it had just one row of the Victorian variety 'Connover's Colossal' – but it was sufficient to gather enough for Ruth to cook in the old way. This was to lay the bundles flat in the saucepan before boiling them in salted water. Ruth believed that this was better than the more modern practice of standing the sticks upright and only three-quarters filling the saucepan with water so that steam would cook the tips. She said if you did this and you didn't watch it all the heads would float off in one direction and the stems would go in another. Ruth (as are many other women who had worked in mansion kitchens) is a great believer of cooking in bundles, particularly leeks and French beans. String had always been available in a brass container on the kitchen table and once tied, vegetables were easier and neater to dish up. Instead of chasing them round the water you simply scooped them out on a perforated slice and cut the bundle once it was in place in the serving dish. With the string cut, the bundle of asparagus had its heads all facing in one direction which was, of course, the correct way of sending them to the table. Before Ruth put the cooked 'Connover's Colossal' into its serving dish she (following the 1850 recipe) got a thick slice of toast 'nicely brown', and placed it into the bottom of the dish. The only accompaniment necessary was a tureen of melted butter.

If asparagus had to be served on a soak-away of toast, spinach too it seems had to be semi-arid. The popular *The Best of Everything* published in 1870 said of spinach, 'it must come to table pretty dry, and it looks well if pressed into a tin mould in the form of a leaf and served with poached eggs.'

This pressed and dry appearance was 'wrought by a wearying process in the kitchen which Ruth remembers well. As spinach leaves boil down to practically nothing, Ruth had to cope with 'mountains of the stuff'.

First it had to be washed (in some kitchens there was a rule to wash it seven times) so that every speck of grit was expelled. Then it was boiled in just a suspicion of water. It took a long time for, as Ruth explained, if you put too much spinach in the saucepan at a time it came out yellowy. Once boiled it had to be transferred to a huge colander and washed straight away under cold water to keep it green. It was then drained in a coarse sieve and wrung out in a cloth. If you were lucky, you got away with chopping it ready for serving; but most households wanted a fine, creamy finish which meant laboriously rubbing it through a sieve. Ruth said this task also took time because you had to try with your wooden mushroom to keep the spinach in the centre of the sieve. If it strayed to the outside, it was difficult to clean the sieve afterwards and the next time you used it whatever you'd sieved ended up decorated with green flecks. Once sieved, the spinach was put back into the saucepan and taken to the range to dry. When it was dry enough, cream and butter could be added and the spinach shaped on the serving dish with a broad knife. If you weren't following the 1870 recipe of a pressed leaf design, an acceptable shape was sloping sides and a flat top, with triangles of fried bread around the sides and poached eggs on the top.

Alison in the vegetable store

Sieving spinach wasn't just an occasional chore. In fact many households had spinach every day, the only exception perhaps being when spinach was served as a soup course. To span the seasons and keep the kitchen supplied, gardeners grew four different kinds. There was the tender, small-leaved sort called 'Prickly Spinach', the spreading 'New Zealand' of which each plant could easily cover a square yard of ground, and two types more well-known today – seakale beet and perpetual spinach.

Victorian hybridists got very excited about their experiments when they tried to perfect Brussels sprouts. At one heady moment, so peculiar were the 'sports' their efforts produced, they predicted a red-coloured sprout. Sprouts were particularly tiresome vegetables to prepare because after cooking each one had to be separated and dried. The usual method was to lay a short line of them in a kitchen cloth called a 'rubber', roll it up and gently squeeze. These were laid in an outer circle. As other sprouts were dried, sprout by sprout the circle was completed and built up into a dome shape.

In contrast the ordinary cabbage was not very popular amongst the gentry. It had a reputation for being bitter and stringy. Anyone cooking a cabbage was advised to boil it in two waters. This diluted the essential oil contained in cabbages which was 'apt to produce bad effects'.

There was, however, one now quite forgotten form of brassica which was accepted. This was the colewort or collard. It was a small cabbage drawn before it hearted and Victorian journalist Shirley Hibberd wrote

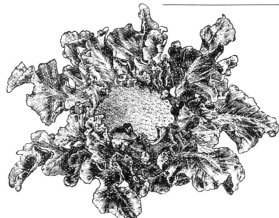

*White broccoli (left) and
St John's Day cabbage.
A nineteenth-century variety*

of it: 'There is nothing in the way of cabbage so elegant or so welcome flavoured as a well served dish of collards of a deep green hue, tender, marrowy, and fragrant.'

Both cauliflower and broccoli were popular in grand houses. By dint of successful sowing a good gardener could keep the kitchen supplied with cauliflower nearly all the year round. Cauliflower was a useful vegetable for it could be served as either a garnish or as a savoury second course. If it was served as a second course the head was often kept intact by wrapping it in butter muslin before boiling. In fact so important was it for the cauliflower not to lose shape that there were complaints that the vegetable was coming to the table so underdone that it was too hard to serve with a spoon. A particularly acerbic critic wrote: 'If cooks and ladies will have their cauliflowers crisp, as they call it, why not serve them *raw*, and then eaters would be aware of them.'

Perhaps the reputation that Victorians have of serving overdone and soggy vegetables is not totally fair. There was certainly a fashion for serving vegetables crisp, for Eliza Acton felt compelled to criticise it and warn readers that the custom ought to be disregarded when health was considered more important than fashion. The book *The Best of Everything* (which in fact was a 'best' itself, selling in excess of 80,000 copies) was, on the other hand, in favour of under-doing vegetables. It told readers:

'Care should be taken not to overdo them, as it spoils their colour, and deprives them of their crispness. They ought to be put in boiling water with a handful of salt in it, and when they begin to sink it is a sign that they are sufficiently done.'

Elderly ladies also tell me that in their experience of cooking in service years ago, if they overcooked vegetables they had to prepare and re-cook them. One said, 'We didn't overcook them as the cottage people would have done – I used to get into trouble when I went home, I never cooked the vegetables enough for them...'

Mr John Barker, a Victorian barrister who liked his food, contributed to an argument about what made a good cook with the sage summing-up that a good cook was a woman who could boil potatoes and melt butter *well*. In fact, Mr Barker never required any more proof of the capabilities of a cook. Such succinct counsel might well have come in handy in a few other contemporary debates, not so much about cooks but about their potatoes. The first concerned whether they ought to be put in hot or cold water. Some potatoes, it seemed, should be put in hot water. These were the small Dutch kinds described as the 'cheesy, waxy roots; some of the inhabitants of London relish'. The dry, mealy potatoes grown in Scotland and Ireland had, however, because of their tendency to fall to pieces, to be put into cold water. Potato skin was the cause of other arguments. One cookery book warned readers that the skin contained cork and the smallest piece if eaten would swell big like cork in the stomach. Skins were variously on or off when it came to boiling time – depending on the persuasion of the writer. There were some who thought that they should be taken off before boiling, others who thought that boiling should take place with them on and that they should only be removed just before being taken to the table and yet others who disagreed with both the above. This third camp argued that paring potatoes at all before they were served made them cold and advocated the method employed by the Irish 'middling classes'. This was to boil the potatoes in their skins and let the dinner guests peel them onto the table beside their plates. In the age of the white damask tablecloth and genteel crumb brush, it is hardly surprising this last method failed to catch on in those parts of the empire more immediate to Windsor.

Households where plain cooking was preferred served potatoes boiled, roasted, fried or with hashed vegetables. In other establishments, variety was everything when it came to this useful tuber. Theodore Garrett, in *The Encyclopaedia of Practical Cookery*, gives instructions for preparing over eighty different potato dishes, from potatoes à la Gastronome to Potato Sandwiches. Under 'C' is 'Crulles', which are potatoes cut round and round until each one resembles a continuous spiralling curl. I met women who in their youth had worked under cooks who asked for a fancy embellishment to these and as kitchenmaids they had to wind the curl around their finger and then tie it in a bow.

With potatoes being served in the dining room several times a day and it being *de rigueur* never to serve them in the same way twice, it's hardly surprising that presentation became inventive. Towards the end of the century it became fashionable to cut potatoes into the shape of an olive. The method was called 'turning', and to do it successfully the position of the hands was all-important, as was having a sharp knife. Ruth, from years

A potato crulle

of experience, is a past master at making potato olives. She always used to keep her small vegetable knife in a little leather belt round her waist. Other girls in the kitchen did the same and woe betide anyone who used another's vegetable knife. The method of making olives is to start halfway up the potato and shape down to a little point at the bottom. This often had to be done several times to get the required shape which was roughly the size of a large Spanish olive. Ruth admitted that you made an awful mess of 'olives' when you first started but got quicker over the years.

As Harry had grown her some quite grotesque shaped potatoes, resurrecting the old skill of making olives would be something of a challenge. It wasn't Harry's fault the potatoes looked as they did – he was only supplying the sort of potatoes a Victorian kitchen would have had to cope with. His nineteenth-century variety 'Champion' was marginally better than its companion 'Lumpers'. Even Harry admitted that 'Lumpers' looked an awful thing with its deep eyes and huge knobbly body. Careful breeding programmes over the years have resulted in today's relatively smooth potatoes.

The same sort of programmes have done similar good things to another 'kitchenmaid's delight' (as Harry calls his knobbliest vegetables) – the Jerusalem artichoke. The old irregular shaped Jerusalem artichokes frequently had to be 'styled' with a vegetable knife. Mrs Marshall, of Marshall's Cookery School fame, recommended cutting them into olives and Alexis Soyer, one-time chef at The Reform Club and probably the most flamboyant and famous of all Victorian chefs, advocated shaping them like a pear but flat at the bottom. He called Jerusalem artichokes 'one of the best and most useful vegetables ever introduced to table, and anything but appreciated as it deserves to be.' He recommended placing them point-up on a border of mashed potato, covering them with a cream sauce and then putting a fine Brussels sprout between each – the contrast between the two vegetables being, he said, 'exceedingly inviting, simple and pretty.'

An awful lot of agony went on in the garden and kitchen before Jerusalem artichokes reached the 'pretty' stage. They are a winter vegetable, and Harry recalls that it was a terrible job digging them up and then having to unthaw the garden tap to wash them before delivering them to the kitchen. Ruth remembers them coming into the kitchen on the worst days of winter. This memory is icily transfixed for she said Jerusalem artichokes had to be washed in the scullery in very cold water. She used to try and sneak a dribble of hot in just to make it bearable but if the cook went by she always put her hand in to test the temperature. If she detected the slightest warmth she made Ruth take the whole lot out and start again so, as Ruth said, you didn't gain a lot really! Once

Jerusalem artichokes

out of the scullery, the artichokes still posed problems. They disintegrated quickly if they weren't watched when boiling and they never all cooked at the same time. Instead of being able to drain them like potatoes, Ruth had to stand by with a skewer and test and extract each one as it was done.

Globe artichokes were just as bad. From Harry's point of view they were wasteful and expensive and the only vegetable where you ended up with more on your plate when you finished than you had when you started. Ruth disliked them too – many houses only served the bottoms but if the whole thing was wanted a lot of time had to be spent in the kitchen clipping all the little leaves all round so that guests would find them easy to handle. Ruth preferred it when Globe artichokes came from Fortnum and Mason – twelve chokes nicely lined up in a bottle.

Below left: Method of preparing artichokes from The Encyclopaedia of Practical Cookery *c. 1890*

Below: Dish of artichokes, plain boiled

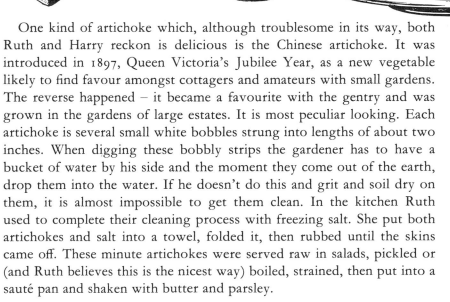

Above: Artichoke bottoms with French beans

One kind of artichoke which, although troublesome in its way, both Ruth and Harry reckon is delicious is the Chinese artichoke. It was introduced in 1897, Queen Victoria's Jubilee Year, as a new vegetable likely to find favour amongst cottagers and amateurs with small gardens. The reverse happened – it became a favourite with the gentry and was grown in the gardens of large estates. It is most peculiar looking. Each artichoke is several small white bobbles strung into lengths of about two inches. When digging these bobbly strips the gardener has to have a bucket of water by his side and the moment they come out of the earth, drop them into the water. If he doesn't do this and grit and soil dry on them, it is almost impossible to get them clean. In the kitchen Ruth used to complete their cleaning process with freezing salt. She put both artichokes and salt into a towel, folded it, then rubbed until the skins came off. These minute artichokes were served raw in salads, pickled or (and Ruth believes this is the nicest way) boiled, strained, then put into a sauté pan and shaken with butter and parsley.

There is, in every Cook's opinion,
No savoury dish without an onion.

At some point early in Queen Victoria's reign this old couplet lost its ring of truth. So shunned did onions become that *The Cottage Gardener* ran several columns on the matter. They began:

Whether it be tyranny of fashion, or a morbid sense of delicacy which has all but banished this valuable bulb from the table of the affluent, we know not, but certainly it does not find its way thither to one-half the extent we are told it does in other countries.

Neglect of the onion was put down to 'fastidious denial'. Onion extract was often used instead of the real thing and even that found its way to the table 'under the guise of something else'. What, isn't said, but it can't have been garlic for that seems to have been even more fastidiously denied than onions. The odoriferous nature of these two bulbs, not only in the mouth but in the kitchen, was a problem. *Kettner's Book of the Table* recommended that instead of frying onions the strong-smelling English way, cooks should do them the French way. This was to shake the rings in flour till well covered, then put them into a wire basket and dip into a frying kettle of hot beef fat for 5 to 6 minutes. After draining, the rings were sprinkled with salt and then served. By Ruth's day it wasn't so much smell as wetness which caused fastidiousness in the dining room. The master of one household always insisted on having his onions dry and his desire for them used to coincide unerringly with Ruth's days off. As the method of achieving dry onions was something that Ruth seemed to have mastered a little more than her companions, before she went out she had to dismantle the cooked onions, put them in a tammy cloth, wring them out tight and then build them back up into onion shapes.

Left to right: Trebons Onion, Garlic, James's Keeping, Naples Giant Rocca

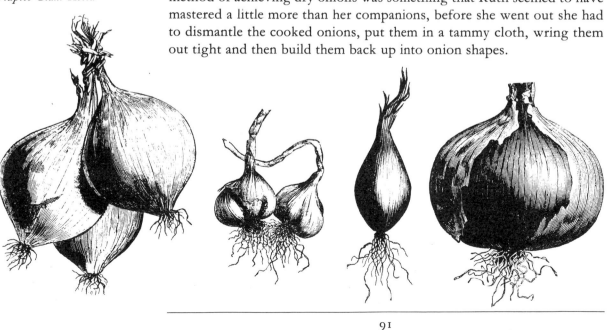

Before leaving vegetables, it's worth noting an interesting twist. Two vegetables, the white-rooted salsify and the black-rooted scorzonera, were grown in Victorian estate gardens and taken to the kitchen in order to give interest and diversity to the winter root crop. Today, with the wealth of imported produce available, we no longer need our winter vegetables enlivened by oddities – but paradoxically, these same two vegetables have been brought back into fashion to do exactly that. They now 'pep' up customer attraction to vegetable counters made boring by all-the-year-round vegetables. Who knows – in desperation one day soon, supermarkets may resurrect that other truly Victorian vegetable oddity, which looks like a giant celery – the cardoon. I've included a recipe for it later, just in case.

Only one cardoon, but Harry needed a wheelbarrow to transport it

CHAPTER SEVEN

Preserving

The July orchard has been put into the January larder

Despite Fortnum and Mason being so proud of their extraordinary rose-coloured honey that they presented a jar of it in 1870 to the South Kensington Museum and despite Edward Pink, Jam Manufacturer of London, saying of his steam-run boilers: 'It is a sight to see all this machinery in motion and to think what a torrent of jam is thrown loose before society', the task of making preserves in the home continued.

Nursery bread and butter, winter dumplings, fritters and puddings were all spread with jams made during the hot, early days of summer. In large houses the housekeeper made all the preserves, working with her maids in the still room. Where there was no housekeeper, the kitchen had to suffer the stifling combined heat of a bubbling jam kettle and a range stoked to cope with other tasks.

If her employer thought it a useful acquisition, a kitchenmaid might have the luxury of a portable stove which could be put out into the cool scullery or onto a table well away from the range. The small French stove recommended by Eliza Acton, which sold for seven shillings, burnt charcoal and had to be placed where there was a free flow of air. Once in place, a baking tray was slipped underneath to catch falling embers. Gas stoves were thought to be best for jam-making – they could give the constant sharp heat needed to save the colour of the fruit. If a kitchen was modern enough to have a gas stove it was quite likely that it also had an enamelled stewpan. If the old copper type was still in use it brought an additional task for this had to be carefully scoured with sand and vinegar, and then well washed and dried before being set onto the stove. Other essentials were a trivet (to help stop the jam burning), sieves, wooden spoons, the actual fruit to be preserved and, as important as the fruit, the right sort of sugar.

Until 1874, only the rich could afford the right sort of sugar. In that year, despite it being a main source of income for the Treasury, Prime Minister Gladstone abolished the Sugar Tax. Prior to this poor people had used cheap, coarse sugar for making preserves. This was adequate for gooseberry jam which set well, and could even be made by using treacle; but for taste and keeping qualities, finer fruits needed better sugar. After the Sugar Tax was lifted many had to weigh their sweet tooth against their conscience; for the demand for sugar was such that to meet it cane sugar was imported from areas still using slave labour. When sugar came into Britain it had to be refined to get rid of fragments of cane and other impurities. To do this it was put into big tanks and mixed with bullocks' blood. When the tanks were heated albumen from the blood carried impurities to the surface where they were skimmed off.

All Victorian manuals recommended using loaf sugar for preserving. To make this, the cleaned sugar from the tanks was filtered through charcoal and then put into conical clay moulds. The moulds were porous and syrup from the sugar seeped through them. So, too, did the concentrated syrup poured through to make the sugar whiter. The loaves in their conical moulds were dried by sugar bakers in large heated warehouses. These warehouses were notorious for catching fire and Martineaus, the last firm to sell sugar loaves in London, ceased to do so in 1893 when part of their premises burnt down. Sugar loaves weighed from 5 to 35 lbs. They were either sold whole or broken up in grocers' shops by large heavy-duty choppers and small 'nippers'. The centrifugal machine which produces the loose sugar crystals we know today was in use in Victorian times (it had been first invented for drying wool in 1837), but crystal sugar seems to have been sold only for putting into coffee.

In 1870 *The Best of Everything* (a volume which was hot on 'best' items) told readers: 'The best and most economical preserves are made with the best fruit and the best sugar'. A century and almost two decades later Ruth Mott, standing in our reconstructed Victorian kitchen, also said (with the benefit of half a century's jam-making experience behind her), 'The secret of preserving is good sugar.' There was obviously no doubt about it: to preserve fruit from Harry's Victorian kitchen garden, we needed good sugar and that sort which the Victorians considered best – loaf sugar.

The indomitable sugar cone and a pair of sugar nippers

As Harry was warning that the soft fruits were almost ready, and as Ruth liked the first pickings because they made the best jam, and as no one could remember having seen a 35 lb cone of sugar on their last visit to the supermarket – we had a problem. David Martin came to the rescue. Amongst the towering and steaming apparatus run by white-suited figures pressing buttons at Tate & Lyle's Sugar Refinery, there is a small corner of history. In it a suspended Victorian metal mould, shaped like a cone, drips syrup. In this, David makes a few sugar cones a year because he's an enthusiast and one day he'd like to see a museum of sugar-related articles set up. He made us a large sugar cone. To avoid damage it travelled

the tortuous route of the London south-east circular and down the M4
carefully wrapped in a towel, in turn cradled in a cardboard box set on
the back seat of a car. Had it been rolled along the road with an iron bar
it would have arrived equally intact – it was so hard.

Apart from telling us that sugar loaf had other names – for instance,
some called it 'Sugar Stone' and others 'Sugar Rock' – old cookery
manuals didn't actually say how to break the cone up into the egg-sized
pieces needed for jam-making. In the end Ruth attacked it with the meat
cleaver. Despite her worn-out shoulders she didn't mind the effort, for
she thought it would make some lovely jam.

Jam-making in a big mansion kitchen was, said Ruth, usually an
afternoon job, because then you weren't in the middle of trying to prepare
a meal and so could give your whole attention to it. It was a job, she
added, that you couldn't anticipate because the gardener brought up the
fruit for preserving when it was ready and you just had to roll up your
sleeves and get on with it, even if you had planned to do something else.
Gooseberries weren't too bad because they would keep a day or two and
in between jobs she could top and tail a few. Strawberries, raspberries and
currants had to be dealt with immediately, particularly if it had been a wet
season. The old recommendation for making a good preserve if the fruit
was watery was to boil it first before adding sugar, as this evaporated a
lot of the water. Ruth's experience was of making jam in batches, 10 lbs
of fruit at a time. This would make about 15 lbs of jam depending on
what sort of jam it was. The next batch would be done when the next lot
of fruit ripened.

Harry had a row of 'Baldwin' blackcurrants in the garden. These were
a very old sort which started life under the name 'Black Naples'. Prior to
the breeding of 'Black Naples', blackcurrants had been small and rather
bitter, valued more as medicine than as a dessert fruit. Much bigger and
sweeter than its predecessors, 'Black Naples' had brought the blackcurrant
onto the Victorian dining-room table.

In an endeavour to keep up a supply for Ruth to use as dessert fruits,
Harry had tried to stagger the individual ripening of the 'Baldwin' bushes.
Retarding fruit was a practice he knew well. By placing fruit trees and
bushes in different parts of the garden they could be made, even if they
were the same variety, to crop earlier or later than each other. The earliest
crops would be in the warm parts, perhaps in a corner by the south-facing
wall, the later ones from trees and bushes planted against the cool north
facing wall at the bottom of the garden. Harry's 'Baldwins' were in one,
long row fairly central in the garden and as thriving bushes, understandably could not be moved. Without the benefit of different locations
to retard them he tried an experiment. Taking instructions from a mid-

nineteenth-century issue of *The Cottage Gardener* he covered several bushes over completely. For this he used the straw mats which, earlier in the year, had protected the peach and nectarine blossoms against frost. At intervals Harry removed the mat wigwams so that the currants would be ripened a little by the sun, then he replaced the covering. When the uncovered bushes had been stripped he started to send the berries from beneath the wigwams to the kitchen. He had, in effect, successfully prolonged the cropping season of the blackcurrants by almost a month; but now the only way of preserving them further was for Ruth to do so with sugar.

Of all the preserves made in the Victorian kitchen blackcurrant jelly was thought to be the most useful. Indeed the *Cottage Gardener* correspondent who had supplied the successful retarding method urged his readers to make some, saying: 'A pint of juice will make a very good store for the winter coughs, and as a pound of sugar does not cost above 6 pence, I strongly recommend anyone who possesses a currant tree to avail themselves of the opportunity of having so nice a medicine at so small a cost.' Ruth was keen on blackcurrant jelly as well, though for slightly different reasons. To ease her heavy workload at preserving time she had always been thankful to avoid topping and tailing blackcurrants. In making jelly there was no need to top and tail the fruit – the stalks were left behind in a cloth when the juice was strained off. As she phlegmatically put it, 'mostly they had to eat blackcurrant jelly if I had anything to do with it.'

Harry performed another very tidy job for Ruth. She intended to follow an 1866 recipe for preserving redcurrants in bunches. The method came from *Complete Every-day Cookery* and necessitated dusting bunches of redcurrants with a feather before tying them onto 6-inch wooden spills. It was a fiddly job but when Harry had finished the wooden spills looked exquisite – the bright red bunches secured with little bows of yellow garden bass, hung like flounced tiers the length of each.

The idea was that by holding the end of each spill the fruit could easily be placed into boiling syrup and then just as easily removed. Then the bunches were cut and dropped into the preserving jars, and covered with a mixture of syrup and currant jelly, which had been boiled and allowed to cool. Ruth was anxious, fearing that she'd end up with a 'two-way preserve' – that is, the fruit at the bottom and the jelly at the top of the jar – but her spirits rose when the currants also obligingly did.

The juice of redcurrants was a useful adjunct when preserving gooseberries. Victorian manuals favoured using red gooseberries for jam and mixing a pint of redcurrant juice to every dozen pounds of fruit. It was the same for raspberry jam, with half a pint of currant juice recommended to every pound of raspberries.

One of the straw wigwams Harry built over the blackcurrant bushes

18 Harry's morning visit to the kitchen's vegetable store. He and Ruth discuss the contents of his basket.

Redcurrants

19 *Vegetables waiting to be prepared on the draining board in the scullery.*

20 *Preserving runner beans in layers of salt. This was a popular method of keeping out-of-season vegetables.*

21 *Ruth using 'nippers' to break down very hard lumps of loaf sugar.*

22 *'Red Dutch' currants growing in Harry's garden.*

23 *Ruth prepares to preserve the redcurrants. The bunches are tied to wooden spills for easy handling.*

24 *After boiling the bunches are snipped off into a glass preserving jar.*

25 *Making jar labels with flour paste and writing paper.*

19

20

21

22

23

24

25

26

27

28

29

30

31

26 and 27 Ruth checking on a Victorian method of preserving and sealing a jar filled with pickled nasturtium seeds.

28 and 29 Peaches growing against the garden wall and bottling peaches in brandy.
30 and 31 Other fruits at their peak and ready for preserving – a basket of 'Victoria' plums and dark red 'Morello' cherries.

32 'The July orchard has been put into the January Larder.'

33 (overleaf) Apple turnovers, raised pie and various cold meats waiting to be packed into the picnic hamper.

34 Cakes, cutlery, fruit and jellies in moulds also formed part of a Victorian picnic.

35 Ruth shows Alison how to prepare food for packing into the picnic hamper.

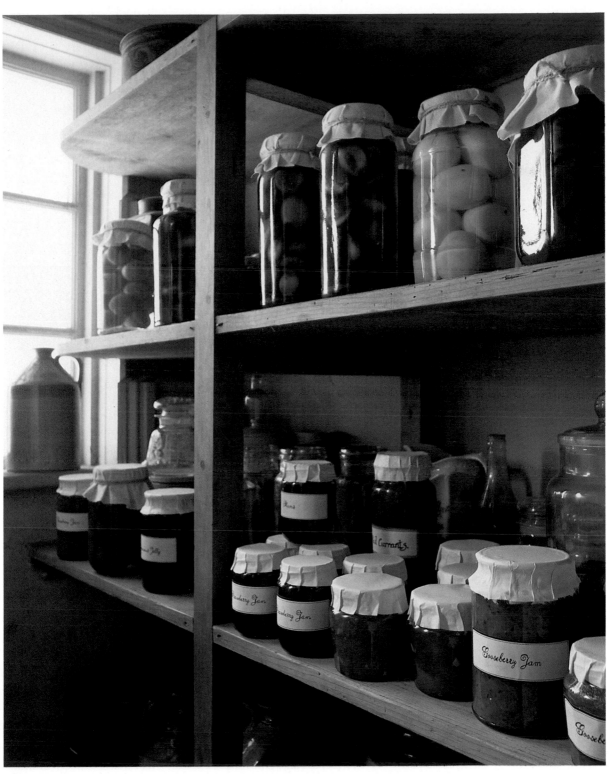

33

34

35

As fresh fruit, raspberries weren't rated highly on the Victorian dessert list and so if not made into jam the berries were used for vinegar. The raspberries were covered with the best vinegar and left to stand for 24 hours, then strained through a piece of flannel and boiled with a thick syrup. It was claimed that the resultant vinegar could, if kept in a cool place, last for years. We weren't sure if the vinegar that Ruth made would last for years, or indeed if the jams would last either. It wouldn't be Ruth's fault. All old preserving recipes finished with the same phrase: keep in a cool, dry place. We had a cool place. There was a large walk-in preserves cupboard in the passage which led away from the wet larder and vegetable store. But like most other parts of the kitchen complex, through years of unuse, the preserves cupboard was damp.

If dampness was a problem, so too was choosing the right method of sealing the jam jars. Eliza Acton recommended brandied paper for stopping mould. *Complete Every-day Cookery* said, cut out papers to the size of the tops and dip them into egg white and that 'Jam covered in this way is quite impervious to the air as if covered with bladder'. *The Encyclopaedia of Practical Cookery* quoted Mr F. Skuse, whom they called 'one of the most experienced Jam-makers in the world'. Mr Skuse believed that dipping paper covers in brandy, vinegar or anything else was old-fashioned, useless and a needless expense. In fact, he even thought the papers themselves unnecessary and recommended lightly oiling the top of the jam with the best white olive or salad oil and leaving it at that. This, written in the 1880s, seemed to us modern folly – particularly as Eliza Acton had said that if jam was left uncovered the inroads of mice would commit havoc in a single night. As Mr Jennings' patent capsules, invented in 1862 (stoppers which resisted attacks of rats, mice and beetles), were no longer available, Ruth finally chose what was recommended as an economical alternative to the paper dipped in brandy method. This was to make some stiff paste with flour and water, spread it over writing paper (the recipe was quite specific about using writing paper) and while the paste was still hot, press the paper onto and around the tops of the jam jars. Had the store cupboard been dry, the preserves probably would have kept, as promised, for years.

Converting the small soft fruits from the garden into jams and jellies had been the best way of preserving them. Larger fruits needed different treatment. Harry had picked and taken to the kitchen some Victoria plums. He'd watched them carefully when they were on the tree and judged the time for picking to be when they took on a lighter colour – 'a sort of transparent glowing look' was how he described it. Tall glass jars, with a green look about the glass and a seam running down their sides where the two halves had been fitted together in the making, were put out, clean

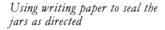

Using writing paper to seal the jars as directed

36 Dairy produce and eggs on the cool, slate shelves in the dry larder.

and dry. The plums were placed in these and covered with cold water. When each jar was full, a cloth or hayband was wrapped around to prevent it touching its companions as several jars were placed into a kettle of cold water to heat but not to boil. Ruth's initial fears over the redcurrants parting company with their syrup, manifested themselves again over the bottling for it seems a similar estrangement could happen. 'Watch when you're bottling', she said, 'because if the heat rises in your old bottling pan too quickly, all the fruit flies up to the top; and if your name's Mott, you turn your bottles upside down and hope it floats the other way in two or three days' time!'

The Victoria was a good bottling plum. It was first raised in a garden in Alderton, Sussex, and put on the market by a nurseryman called Mr Denyer. In 1844 Mr Denyer was selling it through his nursery at Brixton in London. Some people called it the Sussex plum, but Mr Denyer doubly ennobled it by calling it first after himself and then after the monarch – 'Denyer's Victoria'. However over the years, as people tended to remember Queen Victoria rather than Mr Denyer, it lost its prefix.

As there were many nineteenth-century methods of sealing jam so, too, were there many ways of bottling. One old book gave an interesting way to bottle green gooseberries. Three grains of rice were put in the bottom of each bottle, which was then filled with berries, adding no water. Each bottle was then plugged with a cork and resin dropped all round the cork. A small hole was made in the cork and the bottles put into a pan of cold water. After boiling quickly for 10 minutes a drop of resin was dripped to seal the holes and, when the water cooled, the bottles lifted out and stored. It was an echo of the first methods of tinning, where a hole was similarly made, then sealed.

For what was called 'ordinary' fruit, one recipe recommended boiling the fruit first in a saucepan, then adding sugar and, while this was warming, popping a burning match into the preserving bottle. The sulphurous acid gas emitted by the match temporarily excluded air and then apparently quickly condensed to form a vacuum into which the fruit had to be poured, hot and quick. Other recipes recommended that a piece of bladder, well soaked beforehand, be put over the jar once it was filled and before it was heated. In boiling, the bladder would rise but sink again when air in the jar was exhausted.

Choice fruit, that is apricots, peaches and greengages, were given the benefit of double-refined sugar and brandy. Each fruit was picked when fully grown but not over-ripe. It was then wiped, pricked full of holes with a fine needle and put into a saucepan of boiling syrup made from the double-refined sugar. The lid of the saucepan was secured and the fruit left to soak in the syrup overnight. Next day it was brought back to the boil, the fruit taken out and drained and the syrup boiled once again. When the syrup cooled the fruit was put into the preserving jar and covered with alternate cups of syrup and brandy. Ruth didn't mind bottling peaches for, unlike raspberries and currants, only a few came into the kitchen at a time.

As choice as the peaches but delivered in a fair quantity were dark red Morello cherries. Harry had picked these from two fan-trained trees spread against the north wall of the garden. Old recipes spoke of having the stalk half cut, but Harry followed his training, delivering them to the kitchen minus any stalk at all. It was a gentlemanly gesture that gardeners of the past always made to housekeepers who preserved Morellos, for leaving the 'strigs' on the tree and removing just the cherries saved the housekeeper's fingers from being soiled. The Morellos were bottled with sugar and brandy. Old recipes revealed that alcohol could enhance other luxury fruits. The finest and largest strawberries were preserved whole in sugar and fine madeira wine. Bunches of grapes, with each individual grape pricked, were put (and they must have used big jars) in layers of a bunch of grapes to a covering of sugar and so on until the jar was full enough to finish off by adding the best white brandy. Even currants could benefit from a teaspoonful of gin.

It can't be said that Victorian fruit preservation lacked variety. Cherries and apricots were simmered in sugar until shrivelled, and then strained and laid to dry in a cool oven or put into a compartment of the fire screen. Once dry they were stored in layers between sheets of paper. Pounded raspberries were boiled until the juice almost dried up, and then patted into cakes which were strewn with sugar and dried in the sun. If drying wasn't enough then there was always boiling in syrup for days on end to make glaces. Angelica, melons, pineapples, pears and even slices of cucumber were glaced. The green colour of the cucumber was kept by adding vine leaves to the preserving pan. Vine leaves were also used to green pickles, for when the jam-making, bottling, drying and glacing of fruit had been completed, the vegetables had to be pickled.

Ruth remembers there being awful commotions on pickling days because the smell of boiling vinegar went all over the house. On the afternoons they pickled onions, Ruth and the other kitchenmaids each stood with a skewer between their teeth like flamenco dancers because that was supposed to stop them crying. It didn't. All the surplus from the garden was preserved – green tomatoes, red tomatoes, marrows, the last of the plums. Ruth said you could make practically anything into chutney. Her Victorian counterparts would have had an extra preserve to make, not so much to mop up surplus but to be a stand-by for flavouring sauces and gravies. In some books this was known as a catsup, in others as a ketchup. Cassell's *Dictionary of Cookery* published in 1876 called ketchup a most valuable addition to the storeroom and something at which a good housekeeper would always look with pride. E. S. Dallas, writing at roughly the same time in *Kettner's Book of the Table*, called it a 'Godsend to Englishmen' and a refuge from bad cookery to which they could fly when their cooks failed. Ketchup could be made from items as diverse as anchovies and elderberries, but the favourites were walnut, tomato and mushroom. Mushroom in particular, because it was thought that its flavour was the nearest to that of meat gravy. Mushroom ketchup was made from large flapped mushrooms, broken up and put into salt for two or three days. The juice was then drained out, mixed with a variety of spices and boiled for several hours before bottling.

As well as being an agent for flavouring, mushroom ketchup had a reputation for being an aid to digestion. Perhaps it was served with boiled tendon, for out of the ninety-seven articles of diet an American doctor had tested in 1823, this took the longest to digest, clocking up five hours and 30 minutes – a good 15 minutes over its nearest rival, roasted pork. The same doctor also discovered that stimulating condiments were injurious to health. Ruth, who was following a Mrs Beeton recipe for tomato ketchup, agreed wholeheartedly. Mrs Beeton's alternative if you had no ready-made chilli vinegar with which to make the ketchup, was to recommend infusing fifty fresh chillies in a pint of vinegar, which Ruth reckoned could easily blow your head off. As well as being strong, the ketchup recipes turned out to be very sharp; obviously tastes have changed.

Mrs Beeton's recipe for pickled nasturtium seeds turned out an exceedingly pretty jar for the store cupboard, despite Ruth thinking that it was a bit heavy-handed with the salt. The nasturtium seeds were a useful homegrown alternative to capers, although the call for capers isn't what it was as boiled mutton sharpened with caper sauce is now a rarity. The leaves of the nasturtium were also pickled, So, surprisingly, was green parsley and an interesting oddity called 'bamboo'. Bamboo was not bamboo as we know it; it was young shoots of elder, presumably cut into short sticks like bamboo, pickled in a mixture of salt, beer, gooseberry vinegar and spices.

Radish pods, mushrooms, beetroots, onions, cauliflowers, cabbages, cucumbers, walnuts and gherkins, all arrived from the garden to be pickled.

Pickling was also a term which some writers gave to the process of salting peas and beans to preserve them. The method was simple – a layer of salt to a layer of vegetables – but we encountered a problem never dreamed of in Victorian times. 'Salting' required block salt – refined, loose salt makes too much liquid. For 260 years block salt, made by evaporating rock salt in the form of strong brine in wooden tubs with holes in the bottom, was manufactured at Northwich in Cheshire. But the last block salt manufacturers, Messrs Thompson Bros, closed down in 1986. Over the past years their biggest customers had been West Africa where because of the humidity, solid blocks of salt were valued. The West Africans can no longer afford block salt so, despite the fact that many believe it tastes better than other salt, cooks better and is better for making preserves, it no longer exists.

Ruth expressed consternation, tinged, it must be said, with a certain amount of underlying relief, at the demise of block salt. She had done her fair share of salting down runner and French beans and couldn't be blamed for not wanting to slice her way through two or three big trug baskets of beans, with a repeat performance a day or two later when the beans and salt had sunk sufficiently to need topping up. However Ruth wasn't to be allowed to hide her light in this respect under a bushel (so to speak). The Salt Museum in Northwich kindly sent down a block of salt which had been used for educational purposes. Countless children had prodded it with their pencils, and before it could be used the pencil pockmarks had to be gouged out. It ended up looking fine and anyway Ruth and Alison had to cut it into thin slabs to crumble down over the huge earthenware tub of French beans they sliced.

A nineteenth century definition of the product of good preserving is: 'Animal and vegetable substances resisting the usual effects of death.' Late in September or early in October, as part of the kitchen's annual preserving regime, pigs were briefly immortalised. The cook would first arrange for their slaughter – in a medium-sized mansion, perhaps one pig a month might be slaughtered for three months. When ready for curing, the meat was rubbed over with salt, using the palms of the hands and fingers. In frosty weather it was often difficult to get the meat to take the salt well. For a succinct account of curing ham I can do no better than to dip into Octavius Morgan's papers and extract the recipe he obtained from Mr Chapman of Alresford on 4 February 1848:

CURING HAMS

Rub the Ham over night with half an ounce of salt which beat fine, then take half a pound of bay salt, half a pound of common salt and half a pound of moist sugar. Boil all up together in a quart of stale beer and pour it over the Ham boiling hot. Keep it turning and basting for three weeks, then dry it.

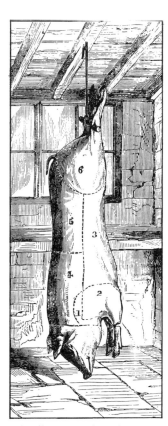

An illustration from A Manual of Domestic Economy, *first published in 1857* 1 Spare rib, 2 Hand, 3 Belly, 4 Fore loin, 5 Hind loin, 6 Leg

In large mansions, hams were turned in salting rooms which contained different-sized stone troughs. The troughs had waste pipes leading to other vessels beneath. This meant that the brine, once drained off, could be re-used. The hams were then dried in the smoking room. This had iron bars overhead and a fireplace outside in which wood, sawdust and peat were burnt. Smoke from the fire came into the room and escaped through regulated frames in the roof.

Bacon was rolled in bran before being hung to smoke. If a house had no smoking room, then the bacon was hung for 6 to 8 hours over burning sawdust or wet straw. An alternative to this was to sew it in coarse cloth and put it in a local baker's chimney for a week. When the meat was taken down from smoking, it was recommended that black pepper be sprinkled over the bone and into the holes to keep it 'safe from hoppers'. After peppering, it was hung up in a thick paper bag.

Gauze-sided hanging meat safe

Uncured meat and game could be kept within the chilly confines of an ice house. A less grand method for preserving a joint in the short term was to wrap it in a cloth and bury it overnight in fresh mould. Even simpler was to either sprinkle it with pepper, or put it beneath a gauze dish cover or into a gauze-sided meat safe. A piece of charcoal placed beneath the wing of birds was thought, because it absorbed gases, to arrest putrefaction. On hot days charcoal was also spread around earthenware vessels holding cooked and uncooked meat.

Hot days also brought more long-term ways of preserving. In summer butter had a delicate flavour because cows were out grazing in the pastures. In winter it became tainted with the taste of turnip, a legacy from the cows' winter diet. To avoid this, butter was potted during the summer into stoneware jars. A layer of crushed salt was placed in the bottom of the jar and the butter pressed down hard with a wooden rammer. When the jars were full, salt was sprinkled on top and the pot lid secured.

It wasn't flavour but economy which dictated that eggs should be preserved in summer. Hens went off lay in winter and shops sold eggs imported from France where the laying season ended in December and began again in February. Despite several hundred thousand cases of eggs arriving through London and Southampton docks, their price in winter was high. To cut down on winter bills, eggs for kitchen use were stored during the summer by putting them into powdered lime or limewater. As this method made the shells brittle, some people preferred instead to rub the eggs all over with lard or gum-water which closed the pores of the shell and kept air out.

The palm for the art of preserving in the Victorian kitchen goes to the person(s) who invented recipes for the following which combined lengthy egg preservation actually within the preservation of something else: 'An Excellent Cake That Will Keep Good a Year' (this contained 5 eggs) and incredibly, 'Everlasting Cheesecake' (which contained 6 eggs).

CHAPTER EIGHT

Shopping

Besides understanding the management of the Spit, the Stewpan and the Rolling Pin, a COMPLETE COOK must know how to go to Market, write legibly and keep Accounts accurately.

Victorian cook in the kitchens of the wealthy could always expect good fresh garden produce, even when she moved with the household to London for the entertainment season. For back at the country estate on several mornings each week, the head gardener wrapped and packed the best vegetables into a large wicker hamper and carefully placed the choicest dessert fruits into specially padded boxes. Labelled and secured, the hamper and boxes were loaded into a trap behind the garden pony and taken to the nearest railway station. The rail service was such that, distance permitting, the cook in London would receive the produce in time for the kitchen staff to prepare the evening meal. Empty hampers were sent back by return.

The recipients of such shuttle-service produce were in the mind of the man who wrote:

None but those who are so happily circumstanced, realise the exceeding luxury of possessing well-grown vegetables brought directly from the garden to the table.

The unhappily circumstanced, with no country garden, had to rely on shopkeepers – especially in London where, unlike Paris, street markets selling fresh fruit and vegetables were rare. Despite an expanding glasshouse industry in the Lea Valley which provided cucumbers, melons, grapes and later tomatoes, and despite the railways bringing vegetables to London from further afield, it was estimated that 95 per cent of London's inhabitants could not obtain fresh green foods on any terms, and those who succeeded paid exorbitant prices. For rarity of fresh produce, the capital was said by one economist of the time, to disgrace a town one fifth of its size. New-laid eggs were as scarce as vegetables. Milk, too, presented a problem. It was distributed in large cities by dairy companies and although it might have been fresh (if somewhat watered down) it sometimes carried disease. In 1873 a great typhoid epidemic in Marylebone was traced back to one person working in a dairy which supplied the distributor.

When it came to buying groceries generally, popular domestic manuals

advised the mistresses of small households to remember the old Spanish proverb: 'He who wants a thing goes for it, he who would miss a thing sends for it.' This was sound advice for despite many small local shops selling inferior goods at inflated prices, servants apparently couldn't be trusted to shop around for the best buy. There was another form of shop which also traded on inflated prices – the truck shop. These were set up by the owners of mines or large manufacturing businesses. Instead of paying their workforce in coin, owners obliged them to take goods to the value of their wages from the truck shop. The benefits to the master were obvious – despite inferior goods, he had an assured custom, he could fix whatever price he liked and no customer had a bad debt because the food bill was deducted directly from his wages. An Act passed in 1831 made truck shops illegal; but as late as 1872 over 150 000 work men were still being forced to use them for, in an endeavour to get round the Act, some employers paid workers in cash but made them wait long periods between payments. When the workers ran out of money the employer advanced them some off their forthcoming wages on condition that the money was spent in his shop. The setting up of co-operatives went some way towards ending truck shop tyranny. Co-operative societes bought goods wholesale and sold them to members at prices below the market level.

Co-operative stores also bit into the custom of other privately owned shops. Fanciful defences for themselves as opposed to co-operatives were put up by small shopkeepers. Writing to *Grocery News*, one such shop-keeper described local shops as ornaments to the town and village shops as instruments for 'teaching the country yokel all about foreign parts'. The picture is poignantly painted for readers:

Hodge, as he stands staring at the general shop of his little village, and scratching his head all the while, is imbibing new ideas and learning something of the dignity of labour and the brotherhood of man.[!]

Fearing that the desire to retain Hodge's window-on-the-world was not enough to make people forsake co-ops, other shopkeepers spoke loudly of co-operative societies coming to grief through fraudulent treasurers and of how co-op customers tired of waiting hours in crowds and had to carry heavy parcels all over the streets of London. It wasn't only parcels in the street. Mrs Jane Ellen Panton went into print to tell how her journeys from town were made a misery by parcels bought by people who *would* shop at the stores. These parcels jammed into her elbows and fell incontinently onto her best bonnet. Despite such purgatorial travel, Mrs Panton was forced to admit that much though she personally disliked them, the new stores, through their competition with small shops, had 'done much for us in lowering the price of grocers.'

Left: Self-respecting butchers displayed sufficient supplies to satisfy the Victorian belief: 'If you want to be strong, eat plenty of meat'

One of the most successful of the big stores and one which ended up supplying groceries to fill the store rooms of the wealthy, was The Army & Navy Co-operative. It was started in 1871 by a small group of army and navy officers. At first it was open only to servicemen and their families, but later membership was extended to civilians. All members were encouraged to pay for goods by a deposit account or cash. This allowed the shop to make prompt payment to its suppliers and get discounts which it passed onto members. Biscuits seem to have been particularly important to the Victorian palate. Biscuit-makers Huntley and Palmer had a huge factory at Reading employing 3000 people and their rivals, Peek Frean, were equally productive. The first Army & Navy catalogue offered twenty-six different kinds of biscuits made by Peek Frean. Many had glorious names like Eugenie, Prince of Wales and Pic Nic. The catalogue also boasted a choice of twenty-four sauces, thirteen soups, twenty-one potted

A grocery shop with ample stock and the means of transporting it

meats, and everything alphabetically between anchovies and (seltzer) water needed to fill the dry larder and pantry. Orders to be delivered by mid-day had to be received no later than 4 pm on the previous day and country members were sent goods in hampers. As customers tended to hang on to empty hampers and not return them, the firm took no chances with the raffia baskets in which they sent fish and poultry but made these unre-turnable and charged a penny for them.

The firm grew to such an extent that it was able to offer additional services for town members, such as sending someone to wind all the house-hold clocks, to deliver theatre tickets or to decant port before dinner.

There were more prosaic advantages to be had from dealing with a big store – groceries purchased from them were less likely to have been adulterated than those bought from a small shop. In 1855 a Parliamentary inquiry had come up with the disturbing fact that nearly everything eaten or drunk in Britain was adulterated and, in many cases, with ingredients prejudicial to human health. An extraordinary variety of bulking-up materials was used. Sulphuric acid was added to vinegar, mahogany sawdust or brickdust to cayenne pepper, tea was mixed with the leaves of British trees like hawthorn or beech, coffee with acorn and peas and a measure of flour could be increased by adding potato starch, plaster of Paris or bone dust.

An Anti-Adulteration Association was formed and in 1872 an Act of Parliament was passed which allowed anyone who suspected an article of food of being adulterated to hand it to an inspector with 'not less than 2 shillings and 6 pence and not more than 10 shillings and 6 pence.' The inspector passed the money and the food to an analyst. The Act met with a mixed reception for it was the poor and lower classes who suffered most from adulterated food and the analysis fees were beyond their pocket. The Act also didn't take into account debased, rather than adulterated foods – for instance, milk that had been skimmed and spices from which oils had been extracted. A more satisfactory Act was finally passed in 1875.

As manufacturers were likely to be prosecuted if their goods were found to be adulterated, many started to put their goods into sealed packages before distributing them to shopkeepers. Like an ill wind, packaging brought the manufacturers some good. The shape and colour of the packet gave an identity to their product and the firm could use space on the packet to assure the customer of its integrity. Placed below these assurances was often a fascimile of the signature of the owner of the firm.

One gentleman who signed his name on such labels with a particularly flamboyant flourish was Justus von Liebig. Professor Liebig was a chemist and in 1847 he had published some scientific papers about his researches into meat. As a result of those researches he started to make what he called

VIEW OF THE LIEBIG COMPANY'S FACTORIES, FRAY BENTOS (URUGUAY)

'Extract of Meat'. The extract was sold for 25 shillings a pound to be diluted in water as a nourishing drink for invalids. However, it was discovered by those who bought the extract that it could also add a good meaty flavour to stews and gravies. A 'convenience' food was born. To meet demand, in 1865 the professor formed the Liebig Company and a huge factory was built in Uruguay. At the factory two thousand oxen, reared in the grazing fields surrounding, were killed every day for seven

This is the ORIGINAL and ONLY Extract of Meat ever guaranteed as GENUINE by Justus von Liebig.

LIEBIG "COMPANY'S" EXTRACT
OF MEAT

AS SUPPLIED TO THE

British, German, French, Russian, Dutch, Italian and other Governments,

HAS BEEN AWARDED

TEN GOLD MEDALS and GRAND DIPLOMAS OF HONOUR (Paris 1867, Two Gold Medals, for best quality, and as FOUNDERS of a NEW BRANCH of INDUSTRY, this being the ORIGINAL LIEBIG'S EXTRACT).

months of each year. From Uruguay the extract went to Antwerp where it was potted up and sent, as Mr Liebig says in a signed statement (so it must be genuine), to 'all the markets of the world.'

At about the same time that Liebig had been pondering the merits of first starting to make his meat extract a Scotsman was experimenting with making new starches for the textile industry in Paisley. The man's name was John Polson and he succeeded in producing a good un-oily starch from corn. This had the advantage of being much cheaper than either sago or rice, normally used, and it was also more suitable for starching buckram, a material Polson's partner, Brown, specialised in. In 1854 Polson patented his extracting process. Up until this time corn had not been popular as a food in Britain because it was difficult to digest. However Polson's oil-free starch presented no digestion problems. Quick to see a market outside the textile industry he called his new product Brown and Polson's Patent Corn Flour and distributed it through grocery shops. Cooks began to use the corn flour for thickening soups and gravies and because it acted as a stiffening agent it became the base of, and helped to popularise the use of, blancmange and custard powders. On the strength (rather literally) of his corn flour, John Polson died a millionaire.

Women benefited too. Blancmange, once a delicacy of the rich, began to appear on the poorest tables and it was far easier and quicker to make custard with powder than to simmer beaten eggs on a temperamental range.

Other commercially made products helped to ease the kitchen workload. Instead of boiling and constantly skimming calves feet to make jelly, women could go out and buy packets of isinglass or, less expensive, packets of gelatine. If you were really decadent you could buy a packet or bottle of Chelsea Jelly, already flavoured, to which you only had to add water. Florador and Rizine made bread rise better than ordinary flour would. Gravine (and, of course, Liebig's Extract) flavoured gravies. Packets of ready-shredded suet spelt goodbye (if you so desired) to chopping and skinning fat bought from the butcher. In winter when eggs were expensive you could buy egg powder instead and, when butter was dear, substitute Butterine. Butterine was made of yellow globules extracted from the fat of newly slaughtered animals. There was a tremendous trade in it in New York and in 1879 almost 500 tons were imported through Liverpool Docks. The origins of Butterine stemmed back to 1870. In that year *The Gardener's Chronicle* titillated its readers with the following oddment:

Artificial Butter – Apparently, astonishing as the idea is, the manufacture of artificial butter (beurre artificiel) is seriously contemplated in France – M. Mège of Paris has taken out a patent – to be used as a substitute for that ordinarily exported to England and Russia. The description of the process is, that animal fat is subjected to great pressure...

In fact, what *The Gardener's Chronicle* didn't tell its readers is even more fascinating. Following the shortages produced by the Franco-Prussian War, the French chemist Mège-Mouries had been competing for a prize offered by Napoleon III for the successful production of a fat which should be as appetising, nutritious and stable as butter. Mège-Mouries won the prize with his invention which was called 'oleomargarine'. As the more commercially named Butterine, the product was bought by unscrupulous dealers and melted and mixed with milk or butter. The mixture, once churned, was difficult to tell from real butter. An Act of Parliament was eventually passed making it compulsory for all imitation butters to be called margarine, with that name plainly marked on the wrapper. Margarine made from vegetable oils and fats didn't come onto the market until as late as 1906.

By calling for a butter substitute Napoleon III had, in a roundabout way, helped the British weekly food bill. His forebear, Napoleon Bonaparte, inspired an invention which was to have an even greater effect on the economy of the Victorian kitchen – tinned foods. To help to feed France's soldiers and sailors during the Napoleonic Wars Bonaparte offered 12,000 francs to anyone who could invent a method of preserving foods. Frenchman Nicholas Appert devised a way. He put food into wide-mouthed glass bottles, corked the bottles down then heated them in boiling water. He was given the 12,000 francs and he published a paper entitled 'The Art of Preserving All Kinds of Animal and Vegetable Substances for Several Years'. In 1810 Englishman, Peter Durand, took the invention a step further by patenting the idea of using, amongst other materials, tin or tinplate as containers for preserved food.

Early cans were made by hand with a pair of shears and a soldering iron but in 1849 can manufacturers stamped out overlapping ends so that solder only appeared on the outside. The first preserved foods were delicacies purchased by the wealthy. The Civil War in America (1861–65) gave the canning industry in the United States a huge boost. This eventually resulted in tinned goods being imported into Britain. In 1863 the Americans canned salmon for the first time on the Sacramento River and in 1869, lobsters in Newfoundland. Although the spread of railways in Britain had made fresh fish more widely available, the imported lobsters (which arrived in tall, 1 lb cans) and salmon were an extraordinary boon to the middle-class hostess. In winter when fresh salmon was scarce, it could fetch as much as 10 shillings a pound but a tin of it cost only one shilling. Salmon was useful because it could be used as a fish course or as an entrée. If it was to be put in a salad, hostesses had to make sure that it was well drained in the kitchen first because if the fish was too moist it gave the game away that it wasn't fresh. A tureen of oyster sauce made

with fresh oysters could cost two shillings, the same sized tureen filled with sauce from tinned oysters cost only 8 pence. The hotel trade made an even bigger saving for by paying 5 shillings they could buy a dozen tins and each tin contained 60 oysters. Tinned sardines and anchovies became favourites at breakfast and luncheon. In 1872 a light-hearted suggestion was made that someone should tin turtles, a food at that time only affordable by the rich who served fresh turtle with cold punch. Tinned turtle became a reality, for in the 1890 edition of Walsh's *Manual of Domestic Economy* it is listed at 18 shillings for a quart tin – sufficient to make soup for a party of up to twenty people.

Perhaps the most dramatic rise of any food imported into Britain during the last half of the nineteenth century was that made by meat. Between January 1871 and January 1872 the total of meat imported (mainly from South America and Australia) quadrupled. In both countries ranchers at first bred cattle for their hides and fat but several factors contributed to making the meat equally marketable. Railways spread, tinning manufacturers set up business and later refrigerated ships were designed. The first of these ships docked in London in August 1877. It had come from New York and had on board 400 sheep and 1200 quarters of beef.

Most meat sent from Australia arrived in hermetically sealed tins. In 1866 the colony sent £320 worth of meat to Britain. In 1871 it sent over half a million pounds' worth. The increase was in response to a demand created by a dramatic rise in the price of fresh meat in Britain. Tinned Australian meat was 100% cheaper than fresh meat, even taking into account the fact that tinned meat arrived without the bone. A calculation substantiates this fact. A 7 lb joint of butcher's meat, bought at 10d. a pound, cost 5s. 10d. After cooking it gave 4 lbs of boneless meat, so cost 1s. 5½d. per pound. Australian cooked meat cost about 7d. a pound, showing a clear gain of 10½d. per pound.

Owing to its cheapness, Australian meat was served in prisons and workhouses. Unfortunately those most likely to benefit from it, the poor and lower classes, viewed it with suspicion believing that it was tins of horse meat. This was a blow to the ruling classes who thought that cheap Australian meat would miraculously lower the rate of crimes committed by ill-fed and ill-conditioned people. Tinned meat was consumed mainly by the lower middle classes. There was one particular criticism levelled at it. W. Mattieu Williams, writing in *The Chemistry of Cookery* in 1885, said that although it appeared to be tender and fell to pieces when touched with a knife, 'the pieces when offered to the teeth present a peculiar resistance to proper mastication' or, as he also put it, had 'a pertinacious fibrosity'. This was put down to the meat having been over-done in the process of tinning. Overcooking was a particular peculiarity of tinned chicken and turkey which had to be served with highly seasoned sauces to make up for lost flavour. As turkeys, pheasants and chickens were tinned whole, the size of some of the tins is to be wondered at.

One of the first vegetables to be tinned was peas. In 1889 a machine was invented which eliminated hand-shelling and caused the market to boom. A disgruntled gardener once wrote: 'Green and blue peas are fully more appreciated at table but on account of the colour only, irrespective of flavour.' It was this liking for green peas which rendered tinned peas a health hazard. The process of putting them into tins made the peas lose their colour and so salts of copper were added to make the peas green. It was the same with all green vegetables. The French, in particular, were guilty of doing this. When the peas were cooked they became a deep unnatural blue-green. There was, however, a moral stand against the practice. Crosse and Blackwell, despite a reduction in sales through people disliking natural uncoloured vegetables, refused to colour their peas.

There was also a brief fashion for pickles which were coloured bright green. The pickling companies let the pickles lie in copper vessels and the vinegar on the pickles absorbed the copper and turned green and highly poisonous at the same time. So many people fell ill from eating green pickles that the fashion declined and no one dared advertise 'green' pickles.

Asparagus was a popular tinned vegetable and from America at $7\frac{1}{2}$d. a tin, American green corn. However, on the whole it was cheaper to buy fresh vegetables when they were in season than to buy tinned ones. If a season was bad, tins did come into their own again. This was particularly evident in 1882 when there was such a poor apple crop that at Christmas the only apples available were a few French ones and 3 lb tins of Newton Pippins from America. Tinned apples were supposed to have distinct advantages in the kitchen: if they were used to make pies there was no need to disturb the pie crust to see if the apples were done, because the apples had already been cooked in the tinning process. The most popular tinned fruits were pears, gooseberries and pineapples. Until the introduction of tinned fruits, fresh pineapples were only grown in the gardens of the wealthy in Britain or brought from abroad on clippers. A fresh pineapple could cost up to 1s. 6d. which was exactly the price given in an 1893 recipe book for all the ingredients needed to make pineapple fritters for six people – one tinned pineapple (whole), one packet of albumen, caster sugar and $\frac{1}{2}$ ounce of butter.

It's a pity that no one found a method of tinning bananas, for these had to be brought in on specially equipped ships and were naturally the most expensive fruit. In fact there was a recipe for a sort of banana substitute which some cooks used. It made 'Apple bananas' and went:

Take apples, peel and core and cut into 8 pieces; sprinkle with sugar, flour and breadcrumbs. Add, if possible, brandy or wine. Fry the apples slices till yellow, then put them into a saucepan containing milk, sugar, breadcrumbs and currants. Boil up and serve hot with sauce.

The benefits of tinned foods were many. In addition to being cheap they were easy to prepare. With the contents already cooked, in many cases all that had to be done in the kitchen was to open the tin and then to put it into hot water to warm the food inside. Tinned condensed milk (the evaporating process was perfected in 1853) cut down on fresh milk and sugar and if required, fed the baby. Having a few tins of different sorts in the cupboard also helped out if you had unexpected guests. Another bonus was that women found tinned foods particularly useful for making entrées. These were side dishes, or as one definition of an entrée puts it, a dish that does not require more than a spoon for both serving and eating. Quenelles were a favourite. They were often made of chicken or veal which had to be pounded before being mixed with butter, eggs and seasoning. Tinned chicken and veal didn't need much pounding. Sweetbreads with tomato sauce or various curries could all come out of tins.

There were, however, drawbacks. Tins could be difficult to open, despite having special knives sold with them for cutting off the tops. If the tin was opened clumsily the contents invariably got broken up. If tins were kept for a long time in a shop which did not have a rapid turnover, they began to rust and pin hole – particularly if the shop was in a smoky, industrial town.

The more tinned goods there became, the more firms tried to cut prices and a lot of inferior produce began to be put into tins, for then, like now, you got what you paid for. Those who paid for gardeners and kitchen staff seldom tasted tinned food. They might, perhaps, be forced to eat the odd tin of pineapple, but all other preserved fruits and vegetables had started life in the house's kitchen garden. As for meat, even by Ruth's day the only tinned meat which came into the kitchens of large houses were big tins of corned beef. The corned beef was eaten for staff supper, not cold but mixed with mashed potato and tomato ketchup and then fried like bubble and squeak. Ruth says they called it 'American hash' and it was a Sunday night favourite.

CHAPTER NINE

Breakfast

It is altogether needless to tell housekeepers that there is no meal so troublesome to arrange and provide for as breakfast.

itchenmaids going about their duties early each morning were blinkered by the confines of the kitchen and scullery. Perhaps it was just as well. For therein busily cleaning and blacking, they were spared the extraordinary sight which proclaimed itself to the morning air, perhaps near the vicinity of the croquet lawn. They were, in a way, the cause of this sight for the growing fashion of dining late had robbed Victorian businessmen of their appetite for breakfast the following morning.

This lack of appetite was bad news for wives whose diet of reading had included Mary Hooper's 1873 *Handbook for the Breakfast Table*. In this they read that, 'men of business should leave their homes in the morning physically fortified against the fatigues of an anxious day'. Indeed, should they not be so fortified, they would eventually suffer a 'malady of incurable character'. In an attempt to allay their wives' fears and engender an appetite for breakfast, some husbands followed the Dr Franklin regime and took a glass of spring water followed by an air-bath. As in taking a normal bath, taking an air-bath meant removing all one's clothes first. However, unlike normal baths which customarily take place indoors, an air-bath was taken outside, for the whole surface of the skin had to be exposed to the influence of the morning air. Such exposure was greatly assisted by friction of the skin.

However the sensibilities of kitchenmaids were spared the sight of the master disporting in the morning air with a loofah for from their cleaning tasks they went on to prepare breakfast. One of their first jobs was to make 'fancy bread'. This was bread rolls (either French or Vienna) and one or more of the following: muffins (baked in a frying pan or on a griddle), crumb muffins (baked the same way but made of stale white breadcrumbs), oat cakes, crumpets, breakfast cake, breakfast biscuits, bannocks, Sally Lunns (unsweetened), Sir Henry Thompson's wholemeal cakes and, less portentous sounding, ordinary scones.

Ruth remembers making breakfast rolls and scones, although her scones on one occasion were far from ordinary. It happened in Scotland where

Griddle

the dance of the night before ended as usual at 5 o'clock in the morning and the kitchenmaids scrambled back just in time to change and make the breakfast rolls and scones. To the cook's fury, Ruth's scones turned out to be interestingly specked with bits of red. In her haste to get into the kitchen Ruth hadn't had time to take off her nail varnish which was one of the first kinds and came off, not with remover but by strips. It stripped very effectively into the scones. From that morning on the cook insisted on inspecting all the kitchenmaids' nails before mixing began.

Victorian mothers favoured cocoa as a breakfast beverage. It was thought to be more nourishing than tea

Ruth baked her fancy bread in an old French oven, specially lit each morning for the job. It was, she said, a great tall structure and to get to the door she went up three steps. The importance of using the right oven was something which had been stressed by A. Kenney Herbert who, in 1894, published a book called *Fifty Breakfasts* – each breakfast designed for a family of six and complete with a plate of fancy bread. Mr Herbert, who in fact called himself 'Wyvern', said that ovens were as variable in their dispositions as human beings and that the old-fashioned kitchen ovens were deficient in bottom heat, an essential feature for the making of bread and cakes. As well as promoting proper ovens, 'Wyvern' also propounded the importance of preparing beforehand. Such preparation would help to provide variety in dishes and relieve the monotony with which bacon and eggs appeared on the breakfast table.

The eggs and bacon monotony also troubled Mrs Beeton (or at least a journalist at her publishers, Ward Lock, for Mrs Beeton had long since died when her *One Shilling Cookery Book* was published). She/he urged cooks to convert scraps of fish, meat and vegetables left over from previous meals into tasty little dishes, such as rissoles, mince and kedgeree. 'Wyvern' went into more detail, advocating a Dutch oven (an open-fronted tin box containing hooks above a drip tray) being placed before the fire to heat gratins and accommodate dishes containing minces and re-cooked fish or eggs. Breadcrumbs and a bottle of well-rasped light-brown crust were also part of the reconstituting armoury, as was the *bain-marie*. The latter could be used to reheat meat and fish set in sauce the night before and hashes, stews and ragouts. One reconstituted dish is a wonderful example of variety and economy working in tandem. If boiled eggs were returned untouched from the breakfast table, next morning they could be re-presented but this time shelled, placed on toast and surrounded by broth or white sauce flavoured with onion.

Eggs broiled or boiled were thought more suitable for breakfast than any other dish. Attractive silver or silver-plated egg-cups in stands complete with attached spoons were as *de rigueur* on the breakfast table, as were fancy bread and preserves. A footman put the egg-stand onto a plate and offered eggs around the table. Sometimes, to keep the eggs hot, they were wrapped in a serviette and the egg-cups placed instead by people's plates. The best eggs for boiling were fresh ones as eggs preserved in lime were likely to have brittle shells which would burst. There were, however, degrees of freshness for in London eggs were classed as fresh even when they were, as one disgusted writer put it, 'an apology for pepper'. The problem of getting fresh eggs increased in winter when hens went off lay and when, because of stockpiling by importers, even the freshness of foreign eggs was dubious.

Egg-stand with spoons for the breakfast table

If it was so difficult to obtain fresh eggs, one wonders how it is that boiled eggs became so popular, especially amongst the gentry. Perhaps it stems back to what the Victorians themselves called 'the most remarkable phenomena of modern times', for just as Britain was swept by Beatle Mania in the 1960s, one hundred years earlier it had experienced 'Poultry Mania'. In 1847 hens known as Cochin Chinas or Shanghaes were brought into Britain. No similar fowl had ever been seen in Europe. They were large (some weighed 12 pounds), gentle, easy to keep and, with feathers extending the length of their legs, extraordinary to look at. Queen Victoria added some Cochins to her poultry collection at Windsor, and so sought after did the breed become that it was not unknown for 100 guineas to be paid for one cock bird. Cochins were credited with furnishing 'eggs for breakfasts, fowls for the table, and better morals than even Dr Watt's hymns for the children, who were from them 'to learn kind and gentle manners and thenceforth to live in peace.' It is uncertain whether they succeeded in furnishing children's morals but they certainly furnished the breakfast table with eggs, for even in winter, Cochins were prolific layers. Victorian records of the number of eggs laid by Cochins have never been equalled. In more recent times poultry experts believe that it was moving the hens from one country to another which prompted them to lay so excessively. Whatever the reason, Cochins were probably largely responsible for securing boiled eggs their place on the nineteenth-century breakfast table.

The Lightning Egg Cutter, Nickel Plated, 12/- doz.

The popularity of boiled eggs brought a rash of egg gadgets. Amongst these were 'The Lightning Egg Cutter' (nickel-plated) for taking the top off an egg, once boiled, and, to help with getting it to the boiled state, 'The Patent Signal Egg Boiler'. This had a lever which could be set at 2, 3 or 4 minutes (depending on how well you wanted your egg done); and

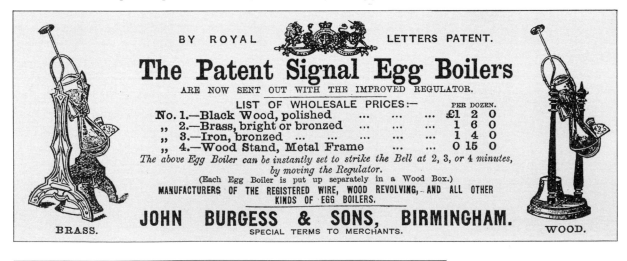

when the sand had run for the chosen time, a small hammer struck a bell on the bottom of the stand.

Mary Hooper (in addition to worrying about businessmen's fatigue through lack of breakfast) worried about egg timers. She believed that it was far better to time eggs from the kitchen clock and keep them boiling, not 'galloping' as some cooks were prone to do, for four minutes for a fresh egg and three minutes for not such a fresh one. Other experts recommended boiling eggs over a methylated spirit lamp, with the eggs being put in when the water boiled. After ten seconds the lamp should be removed, the saucepan lid put on and the egg left for 8 minutes. Soft and easily digestible seem to have been the merits required of a boiled egg.

The task of making omelettes seems to have presented difficulties. According to one source, breakfast omelettes usually wavered between being the consistency of leather or being so raw on the inside that they were 'unpleasant to persons of delicate appetite'. On the whole, omelettes were unpopular and troublesome for the kitchen staff. Ruth worked for a cook who made five omelettes before having one accepted. It was the first she'd sent up, and in desperation she had re-submitted it.

Two other breakfast staples also remained troublesome over the years. The first was bacon. In Victorian eyes it was either over- or under-cooked, too salty, too new, too fatty or too expensive. Ruth's employers always returned it if it wasn't crunchy. Ruth says she doesn't know what they'd do if they were alive today, because it's impossible now to get bacon that will crunch properly. When she was in service she used to do it by putting the bacon onto a baking tray and popping it into the oven. The other *bête noire* was sausages. If they weren't constantly turned they developed a white line and that, said Ruth, never went down well. In fact the trauma of having to have lineless sausages so affected one retired kitchenmaid, that even now, fifty years on, when cooking them for herself and her

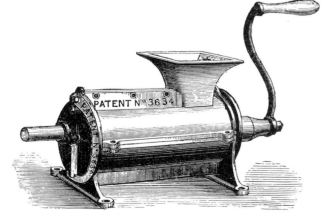

Sausage machine

husband she worries if one develops a white line. It wasn't just white lines which worried nineteenth-century breakfasters – it was what might be inside the sausage. Their contents were a delicate subject to approach in decent cookery books. No one had the power to examine a sausage-maker's premises and, particularly in big manufacturing towns, large quantities of diseased meat went in through their doors and went out again as sausages. Only sausages made at home could be guaranteed as wholesome. Shops sold sausage machines which fixed onto the edge of the kitchen table like a coffee mill, and tins of sausage skins.

In the first edition of her cookery book, Mrs Beeton recommended baked mushrooms as a breakfast dish. Ruth followed this recipe which was delicious but simple: just put a knob of butter and some pepper on each mushroom and bake them for twenty minutes.

The simplicity of the dish belied the work it took in getting the mushrooms to the kitchen. The mushroom house at Harry's garden had long ago lost its tiered beds, housing instead a generator at one end and a motley collection of wood at the other. Harry decided to grow mushrooms for the kitchen on a ridge – it had been done like that in Victorian days and he'd caught a glimpse of the tail-end of the practice in 1937. The old darkened 'forcing' house behind the south wall of the garden was empty, so he carefully laid out a ridge of fermented manure on its stone floor. When the manure had cooled sufficiently he put in the mushroom spawn and then collected a wheelbarrow full of soil from mole hills (the fine tilth was ideal for 'capping' or covering the bed). The ridge lay solemnly in the gloom like a neolithic burial mound. Harry kept a close eye on it, as watering was crucial. In three weeks tiny white spots began to appear through the mole tilth. They grew with such rapidity that the ridge took on a startling luminosity, so covered was it with the white caps of scores of mushrooms. Harry was delighted. He said it endorsed how clever the old boys had been, because you got a far greater area of bed by making a ridge than you would have done by spreading the manure flat on the floor.

The cooking of mushrooms raised on artificial beds was brought about for two reasons. The first was that alarm had been spread at the number of fatal accidents caused by people eating poisonous wild fungi which they gathered thinking them mushrooms. This wasn't helped if the kitchen had a French chef, for there was a popular belief that no sort of mushroom would poison a Frenchman. The second reason was that regularly spawned beds could, if carefully managed, keep up an almost constant supply of mushrooms to the kitchen – a boon for the cook who was always looking for variety in tasty dishes.

Fresh fish seldom appeared at Victorian breakfasts, possibly because of a dislike for keeping it overnight. If it was kept, a teaspoonful of vinegar was poured into a dish and the fish pulled back and front through it to help to preserve it. Fresh sole was an occasional luxury in small households, but if fish *was* served at breakfast, it was generally left over from dinner or dried, smoked or tinned. Despite its popularity it was acknowledged that dried fish did have drawbacks – it wasn't wholesome and it wasn't cheap. The best way of preparing it was to pour boiling water over it in a basin, cover the basin with a plate, let it stand for five minutes then take it out and put it on a hot dish before the fire and rub it over with butter.

Ornamental sardine-box

Ruth was taught the best way of dealing with smoked kippers. When the range was lit in the morning, the back of each kipper was held against the hot range top – just for a second. This was sufficient to cook the skin and make it easy to peel off, instead of, as she said, staggering about trying to remove it with a knife.

The choice of meat dishes suitable for breakfast was immense. Of the cold meats (which stood on the sideboard beside the breakfast table) there could be tongue, ham, beef, brawn and game pie, not to mention pork pies and potted meats. Hot meats could include chicken (boiled or fried), sheep's brains, sheep's tongues (these could also be served cold and glazed), fried rabbit, sweetbreads, roulades of mutton or beef, fillet steak, rump steak, mutton chop, kidneys, bacon, roast partridges, pigeons, woodcocks or quails, curry of mutton, dry hashed mutton, quenelles (dainty shapes of forcemeat), cowheel with tomato sauce (or gravy) and cromeskies (a kind of fritter). One dish which I suppose would have come under meat was marrow toast. This was bone marrow boiled, strained and spread on thin toast before being put before the fire for a few minutes and then sprinkled with pepper, salt and parsley and served very hot.

The amount of meat served at breakfast depended on the wealth of the family. Large houses might have a choice of three cold dishes (for example, game pie, a round of beef and a ham), with perhaps kidneys, bacon and mutton cutlets as hot meats. According to one late Victorian domestic manual, it would be proper for a family of moderate means entertaining guests in winter to serve cold pressed beef, salmis of game and devilled turkey at breakfast. On a day when guests were not present they might have only one meat dish – for example, grilled bacon or broiled kidneys. For families with what the manual described as an 'economical' budget, it was suggested that meat appear on the breakfast table on only a few days each week in the form of rissoles made from left-over meat scraps or, equally modest, kidney toast.

Breakfast toast, whether buttered or dry, had to be prepared not longer than five or six minutes before serving. Buttered toast was placed on a hot water plate; dry toast in a rack. Ruth was always late with toast, she never knew why. Perhaps it was because she stopped to see to other jobs, but invariably when it came to the toast the footman was stamping his feet for it. 'Wyvern', in his epic *Fifty Breakfasts*, called toast, 'A very simple thing to be sure, yet how often is it maltreated, scorched outside, spongy within and flabby?' His picture of it being properly prepared, 'a little distance from clear smokeless embers, patiently', bears little resemblance to Ruth's version. She said toast was one of the worst jobs in the kitchen, especially in summer. To make it she had to let down the fire grate and stand in front of it with the bread fixed onto the end of a toasting

Toast-rack

fork. The slice frequently curled so she had to take it off and put it on back to front to make it curl back out straight, and all the while the heat made her face bright red and shiny and sweat saturated her dress and made her hair go lank. She often toasted bread three times a day, for breakfast, luncheon and again for dinner. What irritated her most was that the biggest part of it used to come back down untouched, but despite this toast always had to be made and sent up.

In some small Victorian households there was a theory that hot buttered toast was bad for you, but this was probably based more out of concern for the housekeeping budget than health grounds, for butter was expensive. Two breakfast dishes which were healthy were watercress and young lettuce. Both were believed to be stimulating and mild laxatives. Fresh fruit was also eaten, bearing in mind the old saying that fruit was 'Gold in the morning, silver at noon, but lead at night.' Porridge, hot or cold and turned out of one big, or several small moulds, was also healthy, particularly for correcting constipation in children and, with the same thought in mind, for anyone taking a long sea voyage. Coffee also acted for the best on bowel behaviour, provided it hadn't been adulterated with chicory. Tradesmen were forbidden by law to mix the two unless asked and any pre-packed had to be labelled 'mixture of coffee and chicory'. The best way to ensure unadulterated coffee was to have it roasted and ground in your kitchen. A Victorian food journal has an interesting account of how one correspondent's mother did this:

She used to buy the berry raw. In the morning she would take a clean frying pan, put a little country fresh butter in it, then about half a pound of berries, and stirred them round and round till the whole is done. This, ground immediately, WAS COFFEE. The process was repeated every third or fourth morning; and the reader may go and do likewise.

From the same correspondent and quite as interesting, is his theory that, if a dastardly act had not been committed, tax-free coffee would be available on everyone's breakfast table. It appears that in the 1820s a farmer in Kent successfully grew a crop of coffee. On the night before it was due to be harvested, however, government excise men burnt it to the ground and no more coffee was allowed to be grown in Britain.

Of other breakfast beverages, cocoa was preferred to tea because it contained cocoa-butter and starch which would make up for the waste that had occurred during the fast of the preceding night and would also maintain the body during the day. Tea *was* drunk at breakfast, for if taken with large quantities of bread and butter or with toast and boiled eggs, it was generally felt that it became more wholesome and less drug-like than when taken on its own.

Coffee percolator

According to *The Servants' Practical Guide* of 1880, the usual time for taking breakfast in a middle-class or well-to-do home was somewhere between 9 and 10 o'clock. Families were lucky if they had a breakfast room, for it was fresh and clean and didn't smell of the previous night's dinner. It helped the servants too, because guests or members of the family who had been out late the night before often failed to put in an appearance at breakfast until much later. If the dining room was used for breakfast, there was a scramble to clear everything away and re-lay it for luncheon.

Family prayers took place a quarter of an hour before breakfast was served. The footman sounded the gong for prayers. Ruth says that in her experience the kitchen had already cooked breakfast by this time. It was kept warm so that when they came back down from prayers all they had to do was get it out and send it up. Before trooping up to prayers they put on clean aprons, combed their hair and straightened their caps.

After prayers the butler carried in the kettle or urn and the footman the tray containing hot dishes (cold dishes were already on the sideboard). The housekeeper would have seen to it that the table was already supplied with preserves and bread and butter. It was customary for the master and mistress not to wait for guests or other members of the family but to sit straight down. The mistress served cups of tea if required and her eldest daughter, or the lady sitting nearest to her right hand, served coffee. The butler enquired what each person wanted to eat, the footman handed it to the butler and the butler then served it. When everyone present had been served, the servants withdrew. Latecomers helped themselves.

In houses where only one servant was kept, he or she brought in the breakfast but did not help to serve it. Food was kept warm by placing it near the fire or in summer, when there was no fire, perhaps in one of the newly invented 'Universal' heaters. A spirit kettle replenished the teapot. After breakfast the mistress of a small house, if she was careful about her laundry bill, did not let the maid crumple up the tablecloth and shake it out of the back door, but instead made her brush it carefully with a crumb brush, and then helped her fold it ready for re-use.

There were two other sorts of Victorian breakfast. The grander of the two was the Wedding Breakfast. There were, however, some who viewed this as mis-named, believing that it should be called Wedding Luncheon, and that it was only the habit of late rising which kept it under the 'breakfast' title. Wedding breakfasts had champagne and wines instead of tea and coffee. The food was similar to that served at ball suppers: soups, entrées, chickens, game, mayonnaise, salad and for sweets, jellies, blancmanges, trifles and cheesecakes. They could be either 'standing up' or 'sitting down'. The difference between the two was that at a standing up breakfast people helped themselves and the speeches were shorter.

The Hunt Breakfast was a social affair of a more masculine kind. It gave the kitchen extra work because the men of the family had a cooked breakfast before they went out (in the cub-hunting season at half past four in the morning!), and then they returned later in the morning with their friends for the Hunt Breakfast proper. This was the same as an ordinary breakfast but had wine, spirits and liqueurs served from the sideboard by the butler. One other difference from an ordinary breakfast was that ladies (riding with or following the hunt) did not benefit from it. If a lady was not acquainted with the family who was giving the breakfast, she did not go into the house. On the other hand, a man who did not know the family went in because etiquette dictated that he could. If the lady *did* know the family she went into the house but had to by-pass the dining room and head for the drawing room where, under the eye of the mistress and with other ladies, she partook of refreshment. It probably wasn't half as substantial or jolly as the dining-room version.

A painting depicting the Melton hunt breakfast by George Charles Lewis

CHAPTER TEN

Luncheon

We scarcely know how to deal with this member of the family of meals.

Victorian gourmets labelled luncheon 'an inconsequent meal'. It wasn't too inconsequent though, if you worked in the kitchens of a family who were rich and idle. Luncheon to them was a small version of the dinner they would eat in the evening – the only difference being the exclusion of soup and fish. It was considered bad form to have either at luncheon, although mayonnaises of fish were accepted and popular. Despite rumblings that animal foods and stimulants eaten both for luncheon and dinner produced disease, this sort of luncheon was too valuable for hostesses to relinquish. It was a wonderful opportunity to show a considerable amount of civility at little expense, especially to those whom you couldn't invite to dinner. These prandial pariahs included single ladies, elderly ladies and those who hadn't been in the neighbourhood very long. In fact there was a sort of open invitation to all ladies, although well-bred ones waited for specific entreaties for their presence. A gentleman dropping in for luncheon was considered 'an acquisition'.

Towards the end of the Victorian era, the spectacle the table provided depended on how fashionable the hostess was. If she was ultra-fashionable the only dishes on the table would be of fruit interspersed with a heavy scattering of vases of flowers. All food dishes would be on a side table and served when the guests were seated. At houses not quite so fashionable, joints of meat would be on the sideboard, cold sweets such as creams and pastry would be placed down the centre of the table, and hot and cold entrées placed before the master and mistress to serve.

As visiting ladies ate luncheon without taking off their bonnets or jackets, food which was easy to handle must have been a blessing. Boneless meats fell into this category and in particular a galantine. Galantine was variously described as a sort of meat-cheese, a dish of solid, boned, freely-seasoned meat and a most elegant form of presenting pressed meat. However it was only served if the house possessed a large kitchen where the cook had time to make it. Galantines were made of a loin of pork covered first by a layer of ham, then by a layer of seasoned sausage meat or other forcemeats. On top of that might go a layer of cooked tongue, pieces of game, pistachio kernels and mushrooms and finally on top of that another layer of forcemeat.

A 'kitchenmaid's leg'

Ruth had made galantines and demonstrated the best way to do them. Instead of loin of pork she first laid out strips of fatty bacon. To prepare the forcemeat, she advised Alison to chop the veal and pork well before putting it into the big pestle and mortar. For, she said, if you don't get all your sinews out before you start you'll never pound the meat, let alone get it through a sieve afterwards. Victorian recipes said that when the various layers of forcemeat, ham, pistachios and so on had been completed, the galantine should be rolled up and put into a cloth. Ruth called this stage the 'kitchenmaid's leg' – tied tightly at both ends it did look rather like a Lucie Attwell character's leg. To make the final shape better, Ruth sewed a seam down the 'leg' where the cloth edges met, because she said just tying it with string in the middle made it bulge. Alison put the sewn-up leg into boiling stock for several hours. When Ruth judged it done and the stock had cooled down, the leg was put onto a baking tray and another baking tray, weighed down with three old flat irons, was placed on top. The compressed leg was then dispatched to cool off in the larder and reappear for disrobing, glazing, and presentation as the 'elegant' galantine.

After partaking of galantine and other delights, the fashionable Victorian luncheon guest withdrew to the drawing room, stayed for not longer than twenty minutes, then asked for their carriages to be summoned and departed. Tea and coffee were never served at luncheon.

If luncheon invitations stated the appointed time as 1 o'clock, this really meant the children's dinner. When children were considered old enough they sat with their parents round the dining-room table at 1 p.m. whilst the nursery footman carried up a tray to their younger brothers and sisters in the nursery. There was always a joint of meat (this sometimes went down for the servants' dinner afterwards) for meat was essential, not the least for its iron content. Making sure that children had a sufficiently healthy quota of iron was a common concern. Some people even felt that the 'new-fangled' silver or electroplated forks (which were replacing steel forks in both nursery and dining room) and the enamelled and tinned saucepans used in the kitchen instead of iron had a detrimental effect. The iron factor was something which Ruth had run into. In one house, she had to take the joint out of the oven after it had been in for almost an hour, and stab it all over with a fork until the blood ran out. The blood was then set aside and poured over the children's dinner. In the meantime the joint ended up fit for only pies and rissoles.

Ruth tried to avoid houses with lots of children. It wasn't that she didn't like them, it was just that she didn't like all the sieving of vegetables she had to do for them. With no tinned baby foods she had to push carrots, turnips, potatoes and as she said, whatever was going, through a sieve. When she left a house which had four children and went to work for a single elderly gentleman she thought that her sieving days were over. Alas, not – he had to have his food sieved to help him digest it. Middle-aged employers were not necessarily a refuge either, for their children used to bring the baby grandchildren on regular extended visits. Sieved or not, vegetables were as important as meat at 1 o'clock luncheon.

Pudding followed. Favourites included rice or other milk puddings, suet puddings (perhaps carrot, plum or fig) boiled or baked, roly-poly, and with the invention of the oven-proof pie-dish in the middle of the nineteenth century, fruit pies. In addition to pies and suet puddings there was a more 'wholesome' way of getting children to eat fruit. A mixture of fruit could be put into a stone jar, sprinkled with Lisbon sugar (sticky brown sugar only partially refined) and then the jar put onto a hot hearth until the fruit was cooked. However this was still considered fairly radical and it was recommended that the fruit be served with stodgy slices of bread and butter or a good helping of rice.

To finish off luncheon, regardless of whether it was the fashionable kind, the 1 o'clock or merely a snack kind of meal, was a luncheon cake. There was a special recipe for a children's version, but containing as it did raisins, currants, peel, nutmegs, almonds and caraway seeds, it seems no less rich than that made for adults.

Luncheon was the most informal of all Victorian meals and even more informal when it was taken outside. The word 'picnic' is, according to one reference book, a corruption and combination of the idea of pecking at knick-knacks or trifles. Picnics are first recorded at the beginning of the nineteenth century when people met at friends' houses to dance and eat or, if the weather was fine, to do the same out in the countryside. Everyone brought their own contribution towards the food but, rather like the display at a wedding reception when there hasn't been a wedding present list, there was often a predominance of goods of the same kind. Eventually it was thought best that one person should organise the food to make sure there was sufficient variety. They had obviously cracked it by 1861 because Mrs Beeton in her *Book of Household Management* certainly has variety in her bill of fare for a Picnic for Forty Persons:

A joint of cold roast beef, a joint of cold boiled beef, 2 ribs of lamb, 2 shoulders of lamb, 4 roast fowls, 2 roast ducks, 1 ham, 1 tongue, 2 veal-and-ham pies, 2 pigeon pies, 6 medium sized lobsters, 1 piece of collared calves head, 18 lettuces, 6 baskets of salad, 6 cucumbers.

Stewed fruit well sweetened and put into glass bottles well corked, 3 or 4 dozen plain pastry biscuits to eat with the stewed fruit, 2 dozen fruit turnovers, 4 dozen cheese cakes, 2 cold cabinet puddings in moulds, a few jam puffs, 1 large cold Christmas pudding (this must be good), a few baskets of fresh fruit, 3 dozen plain biscuits, a piece of cheese, 6 lbs of butter (this, of course, includes the butter for tea), 4 quartern loaves of household bread, 3 dozen rolls, 6 loaves of tin bread (for tea), 2 plain plum cakes, 2 pound cakes, 2 sponge cakes, a tin of mixed biscuits, $\frac{1}{2}$ lb of tea. Coffee is not suitable for a picnic, being difficult to make.

Amongst the 'Things Not to be Forgotten at a Picnic' Mrs Beeton lists a bottle of mint sauce, salad dressing, vinegar, mustard and a stick of horseradish. The horseradish was obviously transported in stick form to get the best of its flavour for, according to *The Reason Why* published in 1869, horseradish had to be scraped just before required because the oil

A riverside picnic, 1870

it contained evaporated so quickly. Otherwise it would taste dry and insipid. This was all very admirable advice, but there are two imponderables. The first is how did they grate horseradish in a ladylike fashion? In Ruth's experience, you invariably end up with tears streaming down your face and dripping off the end of your nose. The second is, how did they get a root of horseradish large enough to grate at all in the picnic season? As Harry said, during the summer the growth on a horseradish was like a piece of cord – put that on a grater and it would go all to pieces. Perhaps mistresses gave very advanced warnings of their picnic dates, as we had to to Harry. He had to take up a root in the autumn, put it aside, then replant it in the spring so that by early the next summer, with the benefit of the top end of previous year's growth, it was big enough.

Queen Victoria went on picnics when she was at Balmoral. Ladies at picnics could sit and sketch the surrounding scenery, whilst the gentlemen foraged for archaeological remains, ferns or fungi. Nature and nature-related collections (flowers, butterflies) were particularly popular in Victorian times. Railway expeditions were made for the purpose and if you didn't plan a picnic lunch on arrival then you had sandwiches en route. (Egg sandwiches were thought to be particularly nourishing.) Soggy sandwiches were not genteel. The best way to make a sandwich for eating on a train was to toast a slice of bread which had been cut slightly thicker than normal and when it had been toasted on both sides to split it and put the filling in the middle.

It was advisable to take your own refreshments, for railway catering was not good, particularly in the early days. The problem was that trains often had an enforced ten-minute stop at stations and, with a captive clientele, the proprietors of the refreshment room found it only too easy to charge high prices for low quality. In fact things got so bad at Swindon that Isambard Kingdom Brunel, the railway engineer and director, was forced to write to the caterers to formally complain. Another famous Victorian put out by railway catering was the chef of the Reform Club, Alexis Soyer. He arrived at a station, fought his way through the crowds to get to the refreshment room and was offered stale toast, over-buttered muffin and coffee as 'bad as any human being could possibly make it ...' Getting back onto the train he found himself in the same carriage as a man who had sensibly brought a small bottle of spirits to refresh himself and who kindly gave Soyer some out of a newly invented gutta-percha goblet. The affront of railway catering, particularly the coffee, combined with the newly invented goblet and its contents, caused Soyer to make the man a promise. To repay the kindness he resolved to try several experiments in an attempt to simplify the method of making coffee then in use. If he was successful he would send his fellow traveller the recipe.

To a man whose inventions had included a stove so portable that it could cook a meal on top of one of the Egyptian pyramids, improving coffee-making was no problem. Soyer sent his fellow traveller the following which he claimed was an entirely new system of making coffee and which had never been introduced to the public:

TO MAKE COFFEE – Put two ounces of ground coffee into a stewpan, which set upon the fire, stirring the powder round with a spoon until quite hot, then pour over a pint of boiling water; cover over closely for five minutes, pass it through a cloth, warm again, and serve.

Soyer included this story in his book *The Modern Housewife or Ménagère*, and felt bound to quote to his readers the traveller's satisfactory reply:

MY DEAR SIR – I have made an experiment of your new receipt for coffee, which you have kindly forwarded to me and beg to acquaint you that I never recollect having tasted better.

    Yours, &c. 'W.C.'

Queen Victoria, Prince Albert and the royal family eating a picnic luncheon at Carn Lochan

Towards the end of Victoria's reign the custom for country-house parties during autumn and winter brought the kitchen another portable meal to deal with – the Shooting Luncheon. Great massacres of specially reared pheasants took place over three days of the week, normally, Tuesday, Wednesday and Thursday. The gentlemen firing the guns, their ladies, and the gun loaders all had to be catered for; and if the head keeper did not organise food for the beaters, then that too had to come from the kitchen with the still room supplying bread.

For the gentry the choice of the first course of luncheon over the three days could include Irish stew, casserole, a huge curry with rice, beef pudding, game pies and hams, potatoes in their jackets and Brussels sprouts. For the second course it might be two or more of the following: spotted dick pudding, plum pudding, apple turnovers, jam puffs, apple dumplings, and, particularly near to Christmas, mince pies. For beverages there would be wine, beer and cider with sloe gin and cherry brandy accompanying plum cake and cheese. All would be served by the butler

A shooting luncheon on Lord Mildmay's estate, Devon

and footmen. If the weather was fine the meal was eaten outside at trestle tables, complete with white cloths. If the weather was dubious a table would be laid in a large room in the gamekeeper's cottage.

The loaders did not like casseroles and stews with their beer so they had big hot joints of meat and jacket potatoes. The beaters had beer and bread and cheese.

The sheer quantity of food required and the need to keep it hot was a problem for the kitchen. Mrs Crosby told me that she was afraid of all the potatoes she had to bake. There would be a couple of hundredweight and she was frightened to death that they would burst when they were baking. She packed them up in huge sacks and skewered the tops together to keep the warmth in. The stews went out in covered pans and specially constructed hot boxes. These were wooden on the outside and inside was filled with padding kept in place by a baize lining. The boxes had one or two compartments to fit metal containers.

There could be as many as sixty beaters to provide with slices of bread cut from 4 lb loaves and six slices of cheese for each man. All the food and drink was loaded into a pony-drawn gig by the kitchen door.

The kitchen sighed with relief when the food departed and when the ladies went out at twelve noon to join the 'guns'. With everyone gone, they could supply the servants' hall and have their own lunch in peace before getting on with preparing dinner. On the first night of the shoot it was traditional for the dining room to have roast pheasant. But large though the dinner parties were, they ate only a minute fraction of the huge 'bag' of pheasants brought back. The rest of the birds were taken off the game cart and hung in outdoor sheds until they were sorted. The majority then went to local fishmongers for selling in the town and the choicest were sent to friends. They were never packed, just sent with a label around their necks. It's a tribute to the old days of the post office that they arrived safely at their destinations. It's also a tribute to their olfactory senses that the post office bothered as Ruth remembered, to return one, very 'high' and several weeks after it had been dispatched. Despite valiant attempts the bird had, for some reason, eluded delivery.

CHAPTER ELEVEN

... that newly invented luxury for ladies, so indispensable for their happiness, and so ruinous for their health – a forenoon tea.

The desire for gossip and relaxation by one woman could effectively cancel out another's enjoyment of the same. On afternoons when grand 'five o'clock teas' took place the cook, instead of drinking tea with her niece or entertaining the grocer to a stronger beverage, was required by the mistress to be on duty in the dining room. Here, dressed in her best, she had to preside over a small side table by the main buffet and dispense the ice creams and water ices she and the head kitchenmaid had prepared many hours earlier. Tall ice glasses were not 'good style' and so beside her she would have a pile of ice plates, paper cups and spoons. The ice was dropped into a paper cup for the lady recipient. It was more often than not a lady for the usual ratio of men to women guests was 5 to 30. Men thought 'five o'clock teas', or 'At Homes' as they were called on invitations, a 'mild form of dissipation'. Ladies, on the other hand, saw them as places to meet friends, make plans for other parties, generally gossip and form new acquaintances. They would only do the latter, however, if their hostess was quite certain that they wanted to be introduced for, like tall ice cream glasses, it was bad form for hostesses to make introductions without being absolutely certain that one lady wanted to be acquainted with another.

Guests arrived from a quarter past four until half past five and such was the desire not to miss out on any five o'clock tea happenings that, according to *Manners and Tone of Good Society*, 'even the most pressed lady socialist looked in for a quarter of an hour or so.' One presumes that, like butterflies, they briefly supped and grazed and flitted on to another At Home.

The stamina it took for ladies to flit to several teas in one afternoon must have been greatly assisted by that rather dangerous stimulant, tea. Tea, according to Victorian chemists, had interesting and discerning qualities for it could act as a stimulant on the sanguineous and yet be a sedative to the nervous. W. Mattieu Williams, a writer of popular science, decried it as a drug whose effect lasted for three to four hours (helpfully, well within the 'flitting' period). He supported his view with comparisons

Tea-urn

on his walking powers, first when tea was drunk, then water. Tea won. It is not known how ladies who never took tea survived, for if nothing else was on offer, like tall ice cream glasses and unwanted introductions, it was not good style to ask for an alternative.

At grand 'five o'clock teas', between bouts of gossip and vocal and instrumental renderings, ladies were escorted to refreshments. This necessitated taking a gentleman's right arm and, as such arms were scarce, it's hardly surprising male escort duty was often described as 'unremitting'. Safely propelled to the buffet the choice presented would be tea and coffee in big silver urns, wine, claret cup, sherry, champagne-cup, cakes, thin bread and butter, fancy biscuits, ices, fruits and sandwiches. To eat the latter three items, it was customary for ladies to take off their gloves. The peculiarities of dress rules was something that Ruth remembered well. When one mistress she worked for had an 'At Home', before her guests arrived she would go upstairs, put her hat on and come back down to sit with her guests, who of course also had their hats on. Ruth also remembered, without too much affection, 'At Home' sandwiches, particularly cucumber ones.

In early Victorian days sandwiches were made only of ham, tongue or beef, not cucumber. Cucumber was thought to be cold and poisonous and an edition of *Punch* even went so far as to publish eleven verses railing against it. The last verse went:

> *So much for cold John Cucumber,*
> *Whom few insides can stand,*
> *Of all Cucurbitaceae*
> *The Worst in Merrie England.*

Above: A patent cucumber slicer with three blades
Left: Family tea provided more cakes and 'knick-knackery' than a formal drawing-room tea

By the 1870s, however, it's likely that John Cucumber was warming himself between two pieces of bread, for at that time a confectioner in Glasgow was boasting that he could make no fewer than one hundred different sorts of sandwiches.

Cucumber sandwiches, Ruth said, always seemed to be wanted on her afternoon off and they were something you couldn't do beforehand because they went soggy. They also took time to prepare. Thin slices of cucumber were spread on a plate and covered with black pepper and salt to draw the water out of them. Each slice then had to be dried and individually laid onto the bread. (It wasn't, Ruth said, like Gentleman's Relish, which you could slap in.) She used to end up starting her afternoon off at quarter past four.

Sir Henry Thompson writing in 1891 called tea 'an invention of comparatively recent date' and thought it an undesirable habit if it was solid enough to spoil 'the coming dinner'. As however luncheon had been at 2 o'clock and dinner wouldn't be until 8 o'clock most houses had some form of tea. A 'family' tea might include sardines, potted meats, muffins and crumpets but in most middle- and upper-class families the normal practice was to have a small tea served in the drawing room. This was much less grand than an 'At Home' but still had its rules. Miss Joan Kerr of Gloucester, who has since sadly died, told me that people were very fussy about making tea and that there was an etiquette about it. Every afternoon, the butler brought her mother a silver tea caddy, teapot and a kettle on a stand with a heater beneath it. The footman brought teacups on a silver tray. Food at drawing-room teas was light: thin bread and butter, jam or honey, and cake. The cake might have been in the form of small Balmorals (which were baked in moulds shaped like corrugated nissen huts), a large madeira or a seed cake. Making seed cakes for tea was hard work for the kitchen. According to some old recipes, kitchen-maids had to beat a rich seed cake mixture for two hours. It then had to be baked for two hours.

Cake tins: Balmoral mould (top) and an ingenious heat-conducting design

Today the distinctive flavour of caraway seeds in cake has fallen out of fashion but Ruth recalls having to make a seed cake every day for one gentleman's tea. He liked the cake sticky and so she used to butter the tin and then sugar it thickly all over so that it had a nice gooey top. She remembers it being a trial to bake cakes if the cook wanted to use the oven at the same time. The cook would arrange the flue damper so that heat was diverted onto her dish, leaving Ruth, as she said, having to make the best that she could of what heat was left on her side. She was always running in and out to see how her cake was cooking. The 1880s saw the introduction of special heat-conducting cake tins. They had a metal cone projecting from the inside base of the tin and they worked on the same principle as Stanley's Patent Heat Conducting skewers which helped cook meat. Ruth had her own way of testing that a cake was done and of checking whether the currants in a fruit cake had risen or sunk alarmingly. She cut a little slice out, had a look at it and if all was well, put some white of egg each side of the slice and pushed it back in. Held nice and tight the slice would settle back into the cake. With sponges, she knew that if one had a straight top it was light but if it had a dent in the top, then the inside was heavy.

As its name suggests, it was Ruth's nineteenth-century predecessors who invented that heavy sort of sponge, the Victoria Sandwich. They added butter to an ordinary sponge mixture, which baked better in two flat tins than in one deep one. The two pieces were then stuck together with a layer of jam. According to Victorian manuals, sponge cakes were made more for the nursery tea table than for the drawing room. This may have been because many children were not allowed to eat currants or sultanas. Miss Lucy Holmes of Madresfield near Malvern, an incredibly active person in her eighties who has only just retired from service, told me that this was the case in one of her early posts. Nursery tea was at 4 o'clock. The children would have spent half an hour on their beds after lunch and then walked around the gardens followed by their little dogs. The children led very restricted lives. They were only allowed out with their nanny and occasionally their parents took them out. Their parents might also have tea with them when it was one of their birthdays. Lucy says that all good cooks made a point of knowing birthdays and if on the day a sponge cake, iced pink and white with flowers on it and 'Best Wishes for a Happy Birthday' together with their name and candle, was brought to the table, the child used to be so delighted.

'Many Happy Returns of the Day', by William Powell Frith

Although cake, bread and butter and jam (stoned specially for the children if it was plum) was the usual nursery tea, Walsh's *Manual of Domestic Economy* says that delicate children should have, surprisingly, a wineglass of homebrewed malt and liquor. This, together with an egg or a piece of meat, restored health to the most delicate children.

Nursery tea kept children going until half-past seven when they had milk and a biscuit before being put to bed. At about the same time as the children were chewing their biscuit (a dubious blessing, as biscuits were known to be not easily digested), adults outside on the lawn might have been making their way in twos and threes towards the house. Behind them, inside the pale evening shadows of a marquee, footmen would be gathering the remains of a tea as grand as any dining-room 'five o'clock'. Champagne, wines, fruit-cups, ices, sandwiches, cakes, and biscuits elegantly spread and as elegantly punctuated by fruit and flowers, had refreshed the participants of an archery party. It was a time when croquet was becoming *passé*, and the cult for lawn tennis teas still in its infancy.

CHAPTER TWELVE

Dinner

Dinner, as the word is now understood, means something more than a satisfying meal....

Towards the end of Victoria's reign, longevity in socialites must have been true evidence of a strong constitution. Not only had their bodies withstood inordinate amounts of food over the years, but their digestive organs must have been frequently impaired by the shocks they encountered in various dining rooms. Invited to dinner in the early days of Victoria's reign, a guest was presented at 7 o'clock with the satisfying sight of the table spread as formally and completely as a chess board. As each course was finished, another one was set out in its place. Although his appetite might have been dulled by having eaten well at home during the middle of the day, and some of the dishes on the table might have become a little cold by the time he got round to them, the guest could stretch forward and consume for upwards of two hours. Substantial dishes they were too: boiled meats, roast meats, hashes, hot puddings, rich cakes and fat meat pies. He and the other diners would then leave the hot smell of dinner and retire to another room to eat a dessert of fresh and preserved fruits.

A few years later the same guest, responding to another invitation for dinner albeit at a slightly later hour (between 8 and 8.30 was then fashionable), might enter the same dining room only to find the table bare. Bare, that is, except for a copious white damask table cloth and a veritable forest of palms, ferns, flowers and decorative trails. Wherever could the food be? Anxious glances would reveal some on a side table and some on a dinner waggon, both surfaces flanked by footmen. This time, instead of sitting down a lady beside a gentleman as happened before, the guest would find himself being requested to sit with all the other gentlemen on one side of the table, facing all the ladies seated on the other side. Such was the preamble to Dîner à la Russe which continued with the footmen serving dishes to guests – one footman to three guests. Instead of the guests withdrawing to another room for dessert, fresh fruit was brought to the table. It hadn't been on there from the beginning of the meal for it might have upset guests with its powerful odour.

On being invited to a different house a week or so later, the same diner might have to forget about Dîner à la Russe and cope instead with Dîner à l'Anglaise. This would be because his host did not have enough servants to hand round dishes. Dîner à l'Anglaise was a mixture of the old method of having dishes on the table (Dîner à la Française) and the new style of having them on a sideboard (à la Russe). This time the dessert fruit might be on the table from the beginning of the meal. The host would help guests to soup, fish, the joint, and the roast; and the hostess would serve the tart and the pudding. The servant would hand round side dishes and vegetables. The guest would have to remember not to ask for potatoes with his fish as he had done in the old days. To do so would have been vulgar, for dinner was now not designed to be filling. Instead it had become a passport to good society from which people should rise 'without a sense of repugnance at the idea of eating more.'

Basket of fruit for a dinner table

The dinner guest would have to suffer more changes as the years progressed. Indoctrinated by trips to the continent made possible by the new railway systems, hostesses increasingly began to favour lighter, more varied, dishes at dinner – although by today's standards the number of courses was still overwhelming. This fashion for lightness and variety was fostered by dining *à la russe*, which enabled the hostess to be liberal without being extravagant. Her guests seeing only the portion on their plate, she could have enough of each thing but not too much of anything. In 1878 Doctor Delamere wrote that the 'English dinner is passing through a revolutionary phase, which is not even yet quite complete or universally adopted.' To assist that revolution Mrs Harriet A. De Salis wrote, some twenty years later, a whole series of *A la Mode* cookery books. Her reason for writing was that: 'The rage for novelty in plats for the table is so great that to produce appetizing dishes has become quite a fine art, as it is a *sine qua non* that the eye as well as the palate should be satisfied.' Such satisfaction bid farewell to the muted browns of boiled and roasted meat. A dinner guest now had to contend with pimentos, brilliant red and green foreign pickles, startling white and yellow slices of egg, pink sprinklings of tongue and black trails of truffles. If his host was modern enough to eschew a substantial joint altogether, his fork toyed instead with dainty cutlets and dishes petrified in aspic. There was one dish, however, which once instituted, did not change. The guest could be certain that, following the new fashion for serving a *hors d'oeuvre* (which happened more in the town than in the country), his dinner would start with soup.

Soup was thought to be particularly suited to being served first because it stimulated the appetites of those whose occupations rendered them 'jaded' by excitement and exhaustion. Such jaded individuals included overworked men of business and statesmen who hadn't eaten properly since breakfast. Soup was viewed also as the keynote of a dinner because it revealed the calibre of the cook to 'whose talent the guest is entrusted'. This being the case, stockpots were closely tended. Gone were the days when, as one writer observed, stockpots were as 'little required in the kitchen as a steam engine'.

The most common way of serving soup was to have a choice of one thick and one clear (consommé). *The Lady's Guide to the Ordering of her Household, and the Economy of the Dinner Table*, written in 1861, instructed cooks to put the stockpot on the day before the dinner party. In Ruth's experience, however, it took three days starting from the day she took liquid stock out of the stockpot to make a good consommé. When ladling out the stock she had to take care to ensure that none of the fatty liquid dropped onto the scrubbed kitchen table. Next day, when the stock was cool, she removed the layer of fat from the top, reheated the liquid and

Left: An elegant dinner party, an illustration from The Graphic, *1890*

cleared it by dropping in egg shells and egg whites. These Ruth stirred in with a whisk, anti-clockwise. She said this made them amalgamate more into the bits of meat which would eventually rise with the shell and whites to the top of the pot. To be sure that all the goodness had been extracted from the meat Ruth didn't skim the risen matter off immediately. Instead she put the pot to one side and allowed all the particles of meat and egg shell to drop down again. She then reheated and repeated the performance, this time letting the meat stay on the surface for an hour and a half before skimming it off. After soaking a cloth in boiling water to make the stock go through quicker, she strained the liquid through it. Finally, the consommé had to be reheated for serving. Fish consommé, in particular, had to be kept a careful eye on, for if any boiled over the smell was terrible. Ruth usually kept a tin of pencil shavings to throw over the range, because their cedar smell covered the fishy smell.

Making thick soup was an equally lengthy business. It involved tammy-ing. As it takes two to tango, it takes two to tammy, and possibly more than two, when arms get tired. Ruth demonstrated the art to Alison. She was following Dr William Kitchiner's 1840 recipe for Spring Soup which finished with the simple words, 'pass it through a tamis, and serve up with fried bread'. A tamis was a piece of cloth of a thickish material, which could be bought by the roll. The idea was that the cloth would act as a strainer. Ruth put a long shallow dish on the kitchen table and gave Alison one end of the cloth to hold and bunch up whilst she did the same to the other. The result was a sort of hammock slung between them over the dish. She then poured the ingredients of the soup – rhubarb, onion, carrot, and ham, all stewed tender in consommé – into the 'hammock'. Ruth told Alison to pull the cloth tight, very tight. Then, using their free hand, they each pushed a wooden spoon with a flattened end away from them and through the soup. The spoons met and kept together, each following the other backwards and forwards, up and down the hammock. With

Below: Tammying (left); a soup tureen (right)

tammying, Ruth said, you have to get a rhythm going. Often it's easier if you put a foot behind you. The cloth has to be kept tight and the spoon straight. It could take up to three-quarters of an hour to push some soups through, she added, and it made your arms ache so much that a kitchenmaid doing another job sometimes 'changed' to give you a rest. The idea was to send perfectly smooth, shiny soup to the table. Privately, many kitchenmaids thought that all the goodness was left in the cloth.

Turbot kettle

Arms aching from tammying would have to muster enough strength to gather up the enormous fish kettles needed for the next course. Of these, there was none more enormous than a fair sized turbot kettle. This diamond-shaped vessel was well used, for turbot was a particular favourite at Victorian dinners. The fish was boiled and served whole. The 'Pheasant of the Sea', as it was also known, had to be seen in its entirety for its beauty to be appreciated. Brillat-Savarin, a writer on food during the first part of the nineteenth century, tells of a turbot so large that it was feared it would have to be cooked in two halves. Brillat-Savarin himself saved the day, by cutting up a fifty bottle hamper and using it as a hurdle on which to lay the enormous turbot. He then put the improvised hurdle over a boiling copper of water, covered it with an inverted wash tub and put sand round the tub to stop steam getting out. Within half an hour the fish was cooked to a nicety.

Having successfully boiled their turbot, Victorian cooks were faced with an imponderable dilemma – on which side should it lay on the serving plate? On its white side, which looked nice garnished, or on its brown side which was meatier and was the natural way it swam in the sea? Most opted for the white side but if the dinner was large enough to warrant serving two turbots, then one could be placed white-side up at one end of the table and the other brown-side up at the other end.

The introduction of Dîner à la Russe was a blessing to some hostesses when it came to the next dinner course – entrées. These made-up dishes, particularly as time went on, were supposed as cookery teacher Mrs Marshall said, to show 'the skill of the cook or the taste of the dinner-giver'. She also said that they were dishes which gave endless scope for design and variety. Unfortunately many cooks were not up to achieving either. One hostess of a dinner-that-failed, dismally described a chicken entrée:

Chicken entrée mould

Slices hardened and coated with a layer of stiffened cream; taste of the coating, pure raw flour. Between each slice is one of tongue – in appearance, part of a boiled shoe-sole; in taste, just what the latter might be supposed to be.

Mercifully, such offerings did not remain for an embarrassing length of time at the table but were whisked away.

The next course was generally more successful as it was a substantial joint of meat – perhaps a sirloin or saddle. Interestingly, at this point the butler made his own culinary contribution for besides vegetables, which of course came from the kitchen, he would serve a salad which he'd made in the butler's pantry half an hour before dinner began. When he wasn't needed the butler stood behind his master's chair and kept a careful eye on the table. As each course progressed he judged the moment to ring the dining-room bell. This was to make sure that no time was lost between courses. To have to wait was considered very bad style and proof of incompetency on the part of the cook. Ruth recalls the importance of working as a team with butlers. An experienced butler would be able to tell how many minutes it was going to be before the last person at the table finished. She said the butler and cook had to work together – if they didn't they were lost.

Salad bowl and servers

It was fashionable for the next course to be a sorbet. This might have been à l'Impériale – pineapple ice with rum in the lower half of the glass, and strawberry ice and champagne above.

The sorbet was light relief before another substantial dish – the roast. If the roast was rabbit or hare, the kitchen staff had to make the dead animal appear as life-like as possible. To do this it was served in a crouching position, complete with tail and, by courtesy of a judiciously placed skewer, with its head on and ears erect. Taking the eyes out of a rabbit was a job which turned the stomach of some kitchenmaids. They tried to do the job with their own eyes shut. If the roast was a turkey, then the kitchen door came into its own. Ruth says that if you look at most old kitchen doors you'll see holes down the edge. This is because a kitchenmaid stood on one side of the door holding the turkey with a cloth wrapped round its leg, and another kitchenmaid stood on the other side of the door and pushed it shut. By pulling the turkey's leg when it was jammed in the door it slit it enough to break the scales and so made it possible to pull out the tendons. Ruth removed chicken tendons by winding them round a skewer. All poultry and game had to be trussed, and if the meat was dry it had to be larded too. This was done by sewing strips of lard across the back or breast. In addition to the succulence given by larding, Victorian gourmets could get poultry stuffed with truffles. These came by rail direct from Paris.

Small birds were also popular for the roast course of dinner. Snipe, woodcock, fieldfare, plovers, ortolans, quails and even larks, all found a place on the bird spit in front of the fire. As they were, in most cases, too tiny to draw, the birds were roasted over slices of buttered toast on which 'the trail' dripped. The toast was then served as a delicacy. These small birds were expensive: what a Victorian host paid for a dinner's worth of ortolans (a guinea apiece) would have paid the scullery maid for a year. The quail came into its own when pheasant wasn't in season and large numbers were imported from Egypt. In the late 1920s they were being imported by a rather quicker method: it wasn't unknown, if a family was wealthy enough, for them to charter a special plane for the purpose.

In 1877 *Kettner's Book of the Table* described vegetables as the weak point of an English dinner. It advised:

Let the cook stick to her boils and her roasts – she probably cannot in the way of meat do better; but let her superadd to her small modicum of accomplishment the very simple craft of cooking vegetables in such a manner that with their own fine flavour they can be eaten by themselves.

This was done at smart dinners, for in a late edition of her *Cookery Book* Mrs Marshall gives Entremets of Vegetables as the proper course to follow roast at dinner.

After consuming their delicately dressed dish of vegetables dinner guests went on to sweet. There was a choice of two. Mrs Marshall waxes lyrical on the topic of sweets:

As Brillat-Savarin has described soup to be the portico of the temple of gastronomy, so may sweets be described as its spire.

A little later, Mrs Marshall recommends sweets be like 'the finishing touches of a toilet, that should be relied on to give that finish which crowns the whole effect.' This was an unfortunate phrase as far as Ruth was concerned for the 'crown' that she made slipped and leaned positively dangerously. It wasn't Ruth's fault, it was a combination of things. Judging by the recipes they left and the collection of moulds still in existence, Victorians seem to have been extremely fond of jellies, so to demonstrate an attractive Victorian sweet, Ruth made a jelly. She used an original nineteenth-century mould, but it was so tall and elaborate that the jelly was top-heavy. It would never have survived the lengthy journey from kitchen to dining room. At a postmortem around the fallen jelly, several thoughts were voiced. Maybe Ruth should have gone through the laborious process (which she knew well) of boiling down calves' feet to extract their gelatine. Even so, commercially made gelatine and isinglass were both in use in Victorian times. Maybe the problem was that today's isinglass is not as strong as its Victorian counterpart. A letter dispatched to the Table Jellies Association enquiring on this point elicited no reply. A final thought was that perhaps fallen jellies aren't a new problem and that some nineteenth-century cooks countered it by using vast amounts of gelatine. This seems to have happened to one Victorian lady who described her dinner-that-failed, for she ends with the ironical remark:

Jelly with fruits inside

... there was one great satisfaction for you – the jelly was not broken; it was stiff enough to have stood even rougher usage than the footman gave it, though he did shake it most unmercifully.

Victorian dinners did not end with jellies, or indeed with savarins or babas. They went on. If the sweet had been looked upon as the ladies' favourite, then the gentlemen came into their own with the savoury that followed. Savouries were also liked by cooks who spent a lot of time making them look appetising. A popular one was marrons en mascarade. This was braised chestnuts, coated with a savoury forcemeat and then half with grated ham and half with grated cheese, served in paper cases, a red and white one in each case.

Ices followed savouries, and when the opaque ice plates and gold ice spoons had been removed the butler superintended the last course – dessert. He took pineapples from their ornamental bed of leaves and cut them into thick slices, placed silver grape scissors on the dish of grapes and made sure that those guests who had strawberries, also had cream.

Beneath the gracefully draped garlands of green Smilax, inter-woven with Stephanotis and waxy pink bells of Lapageria, those with any appetite left could reach for crystallised fruits, sweetmeats, and nuts from dishes lined with brown fronds of bracken. By this stage the cook's carefully written French menus, so important at the beginning of the evening, would have become lost in the shadows of the tall epergnes.

CHAPTER THIRTEEN

Supper

Neatness, garnishing, sending up cut papers and other devices may give a comfortable, finished look to the simplest dish.

When it became fashionable to give late dinners, it became unfashionable to have hot suppers. The three bywords of a good supper were: light, wholesome and attractive. Those concerned with their health took this to extremes: for them 'a small quantity of the newly introduced cornflour, boiled with milk' was supper enough. Others, less abstemious, sat down to sandwiches, poached eggs, potted meats, oyster patties, radishes (which were deemed to be very tasty with bread and butter and cold meat), seakale or asparagus on toast, salads, tongue, cold pies, toasted cheese (nicely browned), celery (thought likely to stimulate amorous inclinations in men) and finally, dried fruits, creams and jellies.

The most likely cold pie to make an appearance at supper would have been pigeon pie. No one could be in any doubt as to the pie's contents, for it was customary to have four, spiky, pigeons' feet sprouting from the crust. These pathetic aerials of communication were a throwback to the days when pies were made not in dishes but shaped like loaves. Grasping the protruding feet made the old sorts of pies easier to eat. There's a theory that the word 'pie' might have have come from this custom, it being a short form of Pied à Pied (feet poking out of the crust).

Supper salads came in various forms. There was a simple sort which was mostly green leaves; lettuce, watercress, mustard and cress (although this might have been young rape for the seeds were cheaper), and in winter, celery, bleached endive and chicory. This simplicity did not extend to the salad dressing. One Victorian writer recorded that the question of what was the best mode of dressing a salad caused family quarrels and was one of the greatest difficulties of modern times. Certainly the immediate ancestors of that writer, had they lived in London, would not have had this difficulty, they would simply have sent for 'The Fashionable Salad-Maker'. This interesting individual was a Frenchman named D'Albignac. On request, he and a servant carrying a mahogany chest called upon persons who wanted their salads dressed. Inside the chest were truffles, caviare, anchovies, ketchup, and various aromatic flavourings. When

Cos lettuce

demand for his salad grew, D'Albignac ordered similar chests to be made and filled. He sold hundreds of them and retired to France with £3000. Not having the benefits of D'Albignac, mid-Victorians were advised to devise their own dressing but be prodigal of oil, prudent with salt and parsimonious with vinegar. In 1872 it was possible to buy ready-made salad mixtures – 7d. for half a pint – but once opened the contents of the bottle soon deteriorated.

Despite the availability of commercially made salad dressings, cooks over the years continued to make their own. It was one of the worst jobs in the kitchen. It could curdle so easily. Mrs Emmit of Peterborough says that an abiding memory of her kitchenmaid days is seeing the cook with a basin on her lap sit for hours patiently adding olive oil to eggs, gently, drop by drop. The cook never divulged her recipe.

It is difficult today to think of a standard mixed salad without visualising it being brightened by red slices of tomato. It would have been as difficult a hundred years ago for anyone to have visualised tomato in salads at all. The tomato was then a fruit thought best suited to ketchups and soups. When green it could be made into chutney, and when over-ripe it was useful for removing stains from white cloths, but in salads – never. Raw tomatoes were considered unhealthy and were never used in English salads until the beginning of this century, perhaps in response to some cookery books printing American salad recipes. Slices of beetroot and strips of pickled cabbage put the colour red into Victorian salads, especially the 'medley' kind. The oddly named 'Salmagundi' was such a salad. It had alternate circular layers of beetroot, egg yolk, watercress, egg white, chopped cold meat and pickled cabbage laid around a centre of blanched lettuce hearts. It was ornamental on the supper table and useful because people could take whichever layer they wanted.

A combination salad was a simple salad with cold meat or fish. Salad with crab or lobster were favourite supper dishes. Lobster had to be served really fresh. There were two tests for this. One was for blue, unboiled lobster, the other for a cooked one. For an uncooked lobster the amount of life left in the unfortunate crustacean could be ascertained by the amount of claw-motion following the pressing of a finger onto its eye. For a cooked lobster things were more tricky – generally the feel of springiness in the tail was the key, but unscrupulous fishmongers had a habit of putting a little wooden skewer into the tail and so this test couldn't be relied upon.

Salmon was another Victorian supper stalwart. In wealthy households it was served fresh and had to be gutted and cleaned in the scullery. Preparing the salmon in this way is something which Mrs Hilda Wright of Chirk remembers with anguish. As a young second kitchenmaid, she

Salmon, a Victorian supper stalwart

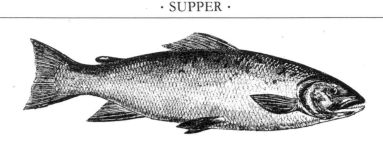

made a terrible mistake. She let a drip of warm water drop from the scullery tap onto the salmon she was cleaning. When Mrs Hardy, the cook, came to collect the cleaned fish, her eagle eye saw the spot (the size of a silver threepenny bit) where the warm water had dripped. 'My goodness, did I get a lecture', Hilda recalled. She never let it happen again.

Having learned her trade in a true Victorian kitchen where spotty salmon were no doubt an anathema, Mrs Hardy would have understood the nineteenth-century dictate that food should look attractive on the supper table.

One spectacular dish was ox tongues shaped into glazed arches. It was an interesting and almost forgotten process which Ruth went to some lengths to demonstrate. She boiled a large tongue until it was cooked and left it to cool in the water so that it didn't dry out. While it was still warm and manœuvrable, she put the tongue onto a wooden board by the kitchen wall and with a rolling pin beneath it pushed the end of the tongue tight against the wall at the same time raising it into an arch. To make the tongue hold its raised position Ruth secured the tip into the board with a fork. Like some faintly macabre work of art, the tongue remained pinioned against the wall until Ruth was sure that even when released it would still retain its arch shape. Glazed and on a plate the tongue looked noble but a difficult dish to cut. In his time the Marquis of Salisbury's Victorian chef, Mr Labaube, got round this problem by inventing a tongue holder. This was a metal frame, bottomless and flexible, and held the tongue in place by virtue of the skewers tightened with nuts shaped like the feathers on arrow flights. This holder was said to be attractive enough to ornament any table, but most cooks preferred risking instability and sending their tongues to table ornamented with the following: a paper frill around the end, slices of beetroot and hard-boiled eggs down the crest, ropes of coloured chopped aspic, a ring of small truffles and mushrooms and the dish marked out with aspic with slices of beetroot in patches and wreathes of parsley outside.

Glaze pot

Garnishing was a serious and time-consuming business, and it's small wonder that before grand ball suppers the master and mistress felt constrained to bother the kitchen as little as possible. The sumptuous refreshments eaten by mildly fatigued dancers at 1 o'clock in the morning would have taken most of the previous day to prepare. To make sure that the dining room was free for the great display of culinary art, the master dined at his club and the mistress ate her meals in a small room in another part of the house. Meanwhile, in the kitchen, real cock's combs were being blanched or artificial ones cut out of ox palates to decorate the cold dishes. Carrots and turnips were cut in the shapes of flowers, and beetroot into diamonds or rounds. Eggs were hard-boiled, pounded or sliced, croûtons made, lemons sliced, button mushrooms, prawns and shrimps cooked and a mound of parsley and watercress put ready to the cook's hand.

But even with the above, garnishing would not be complete without attelettes. Attelettes were skewers. If not made of silver they were thickly electroplated. They had beautiful and ornamental heads, often appropriate to the dish they were destined to decorate. The French chef Urbain Dubois called them *hâtelets* and drew an analogy with the rich jewels a lady wore on festival days. He said *hâtelets*, being the diamonds of cookery, ought to be shown only on solemn occasions and applied to pieces worthy of such an honour. Cooks and chefs placed attelettes as conspicuously as possible on the dishes they decorated. On joints the skewers were threaded with shapes of aspic jelly and on cold meats, with cock's combs, mushrooms, truffles and crayfish. There were even special cylindrical moulds which fitted round the shaft of the skewer and into which small ornamental cuttings of vegetables were dropped and covered with clear jelly. When the moulds were slipped off the vegetables clung brightly in their clear prisons.

Attelettes

Putting crystallised fruits, preserved violets and cherries onto attelettes destined to decorate jellies must have been a fiddly task but at least it created less of a palaver in the kitchen than the making of another ornamental topping for sweets – spun sugar. To spin sugar, it has to be boiled first. Without the aid of modern thermometers, sugar-boiling was a matter of eye and feel. Some Victorian cookery books divide boiling sugar into seven degrees – the seventh degree being the temparature sugar had to reach to be capable of being spun. Beside her boiling sugar saucepan, the cook had a basin filled with cold water and ice. When she thought that the sugar looked as though it had reached the right temperature she dipped her finger first into the ice water, then into the boiling sugar and then quickly back into the cold water. She then tasted the sugar stuck to her finger: if it didn't stick to her teeth, it had reached the seventh degree. The next stage was to take a wooden spoon with an oiled handle and two forks tied together with their prongs turned outwards. The forks were dipped lightly into the sugar and the sugar run from them onto the spoon handle. If all went well the sugar fell into long silken threads which could be gathered up to garnish supper sweets.

Ruth used to spin sugar but she used a rolling pin instead of a wooden spoon. She said you needed height to get nice long threads so kitchenmaids used to stand on the kitchen table. The surrounding floor had to be covered with paper beforehand, because flicking the strands was a messy job. Ruth vividly remembers having to have a great lump of caramel cut out of her hair.

The lofty process of spinning sugar to make a decorative topping

By the time the music struck up at Victorian supper balls, the attelettes were safely in place, the sugar spun, the fancy borders resplendent around each dish and champagne ready in quantity. The kitchen had even organised supper for the musicians, cold meats and beer, the beer being particularly necessary if the band was a military one with wind instruments. Supper was served for two-and-a-half hours, but food though diminished was available until 3 o'clock. Supplies of champagne were never supposed to dry up.

The extravagance of grand supper balls lingered on into this century. Ruth says that all large houses used to have a ballroom and that if a chef was brought in for the occasion he would bring his friends to help. Balls were hard work for the kitchen staff – one day merged into the next and into the day after that. Ruth recalls that by the early hours of the morning she used to be flagging. By this time all the rubbish bins were full to the brim and on one occasion instructions were given to fill up a small outhouse instead. Ruth opened the door to this and threw her bucket of orange peel and onions over a policeman who was sitting inside having a surreptitious glass of champagne. When he rose, spluttering, she rushed back to the kitchen table and tried to look as though she hadn't moved from that spot. At four in the morning the kitchen made scrambled eggs, bacon and kidneys for all the guests and then went on with the new day's work. Despite the long hours Ruth says: 'I'm glad I was born in time to see that sort of thing, because it will never be the same again, ever.'

CHAPTER FOURTEEN

·

Beverages

The subject of drinks is so important and so closely allied to the food subject that a few words on it may not be out of place here.

Victorian women had a drink problem – both in the kitchen and 'upstairs'. The problem was, what could they drink? Many kitchenmaids didn't care for beer, even in small households where with no men the cook could give out good, rather than weak beer. The beverage became even less appetising when it was saved from one meal to the next by dropping a burnt crust into the jug. Some mistresses maintained that beer was not necessary for women servants and offered milk as an alternative. On a muggy day in summer, the appeal of a glass of tainted milk must have been minimal. As tea, if it was allowed, was rationed, this only left water. The purity of Victorian water was dubious. A popular volume of domestic hints felt it necessary to include the following water tests: if a penknife dipped into water turns yellow, there is copper in the water; if a small quantity of sulphuric acid is dropped in and the water turns black, then it is contaminated with vegetable and animal matter. In an attempt to combat impurities water for drinking was filtered and boiled. This made it as palatable as flat beer or tepid milk.

It was the same for women upstairs. Women weren't expected to take drink seriously. Thackeray, writing in Fitz-Boodles Papers on the subject that women cannot dine, said:

No: taken as a rule, women have no real appetites. They are children in a gourmandizing way ... They would take a sip of Malmsey, and would drink currant wine just as happily if that accursed liquor were presented to them by the butler. They are not made for eating and drinking; or, if they make a pretence of it, become downright odious.

In an effort not to be considered odious many Victorian ladies had tumblers, not wine glasses, placed by their plates. This was so that they could mix water with their claret or sherry. The writer Jane Ellen Panton acknowledged that the problem of having a suitable pleasant beverage for women harassed her mentally. She wrote: 'if some genius would invent something cheap, healthy, palatable, and without alcohol in it, I for one will patronize him largely and give him honourable mention, if not a medal, all to himself.' No such genius did and when not drinking diluted wines ladies relied on their kitchens to send up jugs of lemonade and barley water. These two home-made beverages continued to be considered suitable staples for ladies well into the first quarter of this century.

In summer ladies could at least look forward to a diversion in beverages with the serving of 'cups'. If there was no butler in the house, the kitchen probably also benefited surreptitiously from cups as it was their responsibility to make them. Cups were thought to be the most welcome and refreshing of all summer drinks given at social gatherings. An essential ingredient in their make-up was sparkling liquor, either champagne or soda water. Other ingredients could be wine, beer, cider or perry. Flavour was given by adding slices of lemon or cucumber, sprigs of mint or borage and perhaps nutmeg or cloves. White wines such as champagne and chablis didn't 'take' these additional flavours as well as red. Claret was considered to make the best wine-cup and for large parties a composite cup called 'judy' could be served. Judy contained champagne, lemons, sugar, a pint of strong cold infusion of green tea, brandy, rum and mint. Owing perhaps to the green tea, this cup was an acquired taste and good hostesses always offered an alternative. There was also a fashion for serving American summer drinks, amongst them gin cocktail, mint julep, and sherry cobbler. Mint julep was prepared by putting mint leaves and wine or spirits into one glass and ice into another glass, then pouring the contents of one glass into the other until the whole was impregnated with the flavour of the mint. The glass containing the mixture was finally embedded in pounded ice in a larger glass and served when it had 'frost-work' on the top. The accepted way of drinking sherry cobbler and gin cocktail was through a straw or a tube of macaroni.

Less formal drinks suitable for summer picnics included Eliza Acton's 'Excellent Portable Lemonade' (one tablespoonful of this was sufficient to flavour a glass of water) and Raspberry or Strawberry vinegars. Summer fruits also found their way into more long-term beverages. An 1870s book devoted to domestic duties gives instructions for making 'A Good Wine of Mixed Fruits'. This contains currants (black, red and white), raspberries, cherries, strawberries and gooseberries. Added to these are marjoram and ginger to give the wine perfume and (presumably to give it punch as well) two quarts of brandy or whisky. Any spare gooseberries could be used to make green gooseberry wine. The tartaric acid in the gooseberries gave this wine a champagne-like quality and when it was bottled in March it was often called 'English Champagne'.

Wine-making was a tedious task. All the fruit had to be bruised, the husks or skins removed and the seeds taken out. The fruit juice was then mixed with water and put into an open-ended vat to ferment. The next task was to strain the liquid through a hair sieve and pour it into a cask.

Mint julep

Some books advised not to put a bung into the cask but instead to block the opening with stiff brown paper covered in paste. This method stopped people forgetting the hole left for the vent peg in a conventional bung. If they forgot it the whole cask spoiled. After six weeks or so a small hole could be bored about halfway up the case and a quill inserted to drain off the wine to check its clarity. A similar hole was made further down the cask to check at what level the wine was still cloudy. The clear top bit was drawn off and put into another cask. It was eventually bottled when the weather was clear and settled.

Almost as time-consuming as wine-making was the making of some liqueurs. Mary Hooper, author of *Little Dinners*, described the one made from peaches or nectarines as 'exceedingly delicate and beautiful'. Her recipe was to put the fruit into a jar, cover it with brandy and secure it with an airtight lid. After a month she recommended the brandy be drained off, stood to clear, then bottled. Meanwhile the peaches were immersed in fresh brandy. When the second brandy was drained off both batches were to be mixed together and syrup sufficient to sweeten, but not to injure the flavour of the fruit, added. A few drops of almond extract also improved the flavour. After it had cleared, the mixture was bottled.

Aerated water was consumed by Victorian men as an antidote to their over-indulgence in food and drink. The water aided the digestion of the one and diluted the heaviness of the other. 'Seltzer' (imported from Selters in Nassau) was a favourite, especially with brandy or wine.

Ladies, who as a rule didn't over-indulge in rich food or strong drink, had their own health problems. The novelist Charles Kingsley, heavy on alliteration but light on gallantry, attributed these problems to silence, stillness and stays. Be that as it may, a good infusion of the right sort of tea worked wonders. There was lime-flower tea for hysteria, linseed tea for shortness of breath, balm and mint tea for nausea, camomile tea for dyspepsia, violet tea for coughs, and an infusion of roses for 'diminishing certain cases of debility common to females'. Ordinary tea or coffee were not recommended for those of a nervous temperament. Far better for them to drink cocoa or cocoa wine which was sold in the stores.

Beverages for those ailing not with fits of the vapours but with the serious illnesses prevalent in nineteenth-century England (cholera, typhus, scarlatina), form a chapter in many a Victorian cookery book. The most simple recipe is for toast water. It is also one which most writers disagree over. Toast water was made by toasting a piece of bread, putting it in a jug with a thin slice of lemon peel and pouring boiling water over it. When cool, the liquid was strained and ready for drinking. Differences of opinion arose over the correct size of the bread to be toasted. Some said the amount should be a quarter of a pound; others recommended cutting only

Aerated water syphon

a thin slice, arguing that if bread was too thick the 'aromatic principle' developed by toasting could not be given off into the water. They could not agree over the colour of the toast either. Some recommended dark brown, others light, saying that the former burns all the nutriments.

Such variations could not be tolerated in the making of beef tea for, as Mrs Black of the West-End School of Cookery in Glasgow said, it particularly required skilful preparation as 'life and returning health often depend upon it'. This elixir was made from small pieces of lean meat, first steeped in cold water to extract the goodness, then gently simmered. One pound of beef made one pint of tea.

Standard tea or coffee became nutritious for invalids when incorporated into a dish called mulled egg. This was fresh eggs, beaten in a breakfast cup with milk and sugar added, then the cup topped up with tea or coffee. A 'Stimulating, Nourishing and Effervescing' drink for all invalids was 'koumiss', which contained butter milk, sweet milk (presumably evaporated) and lump sugar. To make it the butter and sweet milk were mixed together and the sugar dissolved into it by pouring the milk from one jug to another for a quarter of an hour. The mixture was covered with muslin and left to stand in a warm corner of the kitchen for twelve hours before being poured into pint bottles and securely corking. The bottles had to lay on their sides and were ready for use after four days.

As there were 'strengthening' drinks for invalids so too were there strengthening drinks for workmen – Stokos, of which the main ingredients were oatmeal and lemon; Cokos, containing oatmeal, cocoa and sugar; and Hopkos (a good harvest drink) made from hops and ginger. These were invented by the Church of England Temperance Society who believed that alcohol diminished muscle power.

CHAPTER FIFTEEN

Charity

Many Children and Little Bread is a Painful Pleasure.

Agricultural wages were lower than all others in the middle of the nineteenth century. The poverty a farm worker endured was made worse by the Enclosures Acts, which excluded him from land on which formerly he would have kept livestock to help to feed his family. To add to his plight the Corn Law (instituted in 1815 and not abolished until 1845) stopped cheap wheat being imported into the country until British corn reached a certain price. As a consequence the price of bread rose to make it a luxury rather than a necessity. Farm workers and their families turned to potatoes as a substitute; but from 1845 onwards potato blight frequently ravaged crops. In the last quarter of Victoria's reign, farmers had even less incentive to pay wages to their workers. Cheap corn and meat imported from America and Australia had driven the British farming industry into a depression which continued until the First World War.

Given the above catalogue of disasters it is little wonder that charitable offerings from the kitchens of big country houses were eagerly accepted. These kitchens made large quantities of nourishing soup which was given to the sick and very poor. Milk puddings, calves foot jelly and occasionally fruit were also distributed. It was the custom in some villages for the family from the mansion to go to church in a pony cart. Before they set off the footman lifted into the back of the cart large, sealed soup containers. The soup was given out after church.

In most parishes the farm workers' children walked up to the mansion once a week. They collected scraps of food, left-over cake and dripping for their mother. The mansion kitchen also provided the cakes, jellies and sandwiches which were given at village school treats. At one Christmas party, which took place in a Devon village at the turn of the century, the children were given an extra treat. The lady from the big house was giving out the presents which were stacked beneath the tree. As she stooped the tree's lighted candles set the long feather in her hat on fire and there was great hilarity when the flames had to be extinguished by the footman with a sponge.

Such personal touches could never attend the charitable meals given to city children although there were brave attempts. In 1866 Mrs Henry Thompson set up in Marylebone, London, the first Children's Dinner Table. If someone gave 3s. 6d. they could have ten tickets to distribute. A child holding one ticket and presenting one penny was given a meal of hot meat and vegetables. Dinners were served on Wednesdays and Saturdays and even if a child was ill dinner would be delivered if the organisers were told before 9 o'clock on the dinner day. The Reverend W. Moore Ede, Rector of Gateshead-on-Tyne, was another pioneer of Children's Dinners. He carried about his own cooking apparatus – a large box of sheet iron, lined with tin plate. In this two gas jets boiled containers large enough to hold thirty gallons.

Cheap food for adults was promoted by the Penny Dinner Movement. At the Australian Meat Agency's London depot, over 1000 people a day could eat a good meat dinner for a penny. And in Goswell Road, 300 mechanics are reported to have dined daily or taken their pennyworth of food home to their wives. Queen Victoria gave the system her patronage.

In addition to providing food there was a general trend towards providing the poor with information. Several tracts and books were published advising how to make nourishing dishes from cheap ingredients. One of these, entitled *Plain Cookery for the Working Classes*, was written by Charles Elme Francatelli, at one time chef to Queen Victoria. It was not well received by the critics. A reviewer in the Athenaeum wrote:

M. Francatelli is throughout much astonished at his own humility in addressing people who have to dangle their mutton on a string when it has to be roasted, for want of a 'meat-jack'.

The critic goes on to be particularly acerbic about three of Francatelli's recipes – as these all appear in the first couple of pages of the book, one wonders how much the critic bothered to read. Perhaps he was in a hurry to get on with reading another book he reviewed in the same column – Mrs Beeton's epic *Household Management*.

Francatelli was not the only grand chef to turn his attention to charity. Alexis Soyer, chef at the Reform Club, wrote *Charitable Cookery or The Poor Man's Regenerator* as a follow-up to his practical experience of cooking for the poor. In 1847 he had helped start a soup kitchen in Leicester Square and invented a soup which he said cost only 3 farthings for a quart. He also went to Dublin and superintended the building of a model kitchen to help feed those starved by the first devastating years of the potato famine. This kitchen provided 5000 meals a day. It was an extraordinary success, but then how could one expect less from a man who had overseen the most famous of all Victorian kitchens – that of the Reform Club.

Cooking a joint of mutton without a meat-jack

CHAPTER SIXTEEN

Alexis Soyer

A Man is not what he Saith, but is what he Doeth.

Alan Riddle, the present head chef at the Reform Club in London, believes that Alexis Soyer has left him a mixed blessing – the size of the club's kitchens. Compared with modern kitchens they are large and pleasant to work in, but walking from one area to another takes time. In Soyer's day, however, space was useful to accommodate the constant stream of visitors, for the Reform Club kitchens were a nineteenth-century tourist attraction. The Viscountess de Malleville became quite carried away with her visit and reporting it in an article in the *Courrier de l'Europe* described the kitchen as, 'spacious as a ball-room, kept in the finest order, and white as a young bride'.

Alexis Soyer had been with the Reform Club for five years before his wonderful new kitchens were built. He was a French emigre who had come to England in 1831 and worked for various noblemen until he became chef de cuisine at the club in 1836. The Reform Club was born in the wake of the Great Parliamentary Reform Bill of 1832. Its founder was Edward Ellice, MP for Coventry. Ellice was a renowned gourmet, so it is likely that he looked favourably on plans for the new kitchens when the club was enlarged. The official architect in charge was Charles Barry but there is little doubt that the inspirational refinements and oddities incorporated into the kitchen came from Alexis Soyer.

If you walk into the kitchens today one of the first things you notice are several large pillars. These support the ceiling, for overhead is the Club's grand marble entrance hall. In the main kitchen two pillars rise beside ranks of shining modern equipment. Had you entered the kitchen in Soyer's day you would have found these two pillars rising from either end of a very odd table. It had twelve irregular sides and was designed by Soyer to give, as he said, 'The utmost facility for the various works of the kitchen, without any one interfering with another'.

Above the table but within reach, Soyer had designed special boxes which contained spices and other flavourings. The boxes formed a band round each pillar and turned on castors so that every compartment was accessible. There were gadgets beneath the table too, such as a pair of

Alexis Soyer

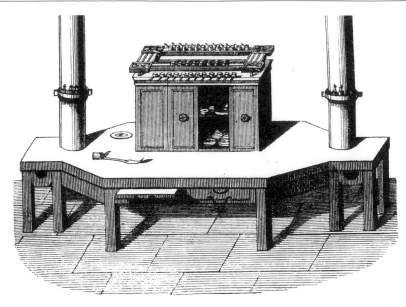

The ingenious kitchen table of the Reform Club

sliding boards which could be pulled out to help strain sauces or give the table extra width. Underneath the boards were two moveable copper buckets filled with water, which were used to wash the table and boards. In the middle of the table there stood a cast-iron steam closet, used by chefs dressing entrées. When they finished, the dish was numbered and popped into the closet until the rest of the order was ready. The result was that the entrée was served as though it had just been dressed.

Soyer's genius for invention appeared in other parts of the kitchen. In the cold meat store there was a meat safe constructed on a new principle which excluded all flies. The door worked on cords and pulleys and could be shut by a jerk of the elbow when hands were full. A dresser in one of the larders had lead-lined drawers. These were used to store jellies and ice creams and there were a larger set beneath used as pickling tubs. Each drawer ran on castors so despite its weight could be easily opened by a kitchenmaid. There was also no drudgery of draining off melted ice by hand. The bottom of the drawers dipped in the middle and ice water ran along the dip into a discharge pipe.

In a passageway dividing kitchens and larders was an inclined white marble slab surrounded by a slate border. On this all the fish brought in for use was kept fresh by a constant sprinkling of iced water from an overhead cistern. The need for coolness prompted another invention – an iron-fronted fire screen which had two folding leaves at each end. When in place the screen completely enclosed a massive fireplace in the roasting kitchen. So effective was it at blocking heat from the huge fire that when visitors came to admire his kitchen Soyer used the screen as a party piece.

37 The tray set for the drawing-room tea.

a

b

c

d

e

f

g

h

38 Taking blackcurrant
ice cream out of a bomb mould.
a and b) Removing the greased
paper from beneath the lid.
c and d) Turning the mould
onto a plate and unscrewing
the base.
e) Blowing onto a piece of
muslin covering the screw hole.
f) The warmth of breath
helps the ice cream slide out of
the mould.
g) Decorating the ice cream with
angelica and crystallised red
and black currants.
h) A crown-shaped attelette
adds the final touch.

39

40

*39 'Five o'clock Tea' –
a good cake was always
provided.*

*40 A tall jelly mould and the
turned-out jelly filled with whole
grapes and strawberries.*

*41 Raspberry jelly surrounded
by red and yellow raspberries.*

41

42 *Ruth demonstrates the art of making stock.*

43 *Ruth and Alison and the time-consuming job of pushing soup through a tammy cloth.*

42

43

44 *Ruth taking the lid off a large copper braising dish.*

45 *Meat and vegetables placed inside the dish.*

46 *Sealing the lid with clay before braising.*

44

45

47 *(overleaf) Dinner-table decorations were part of the head gardener's duties. Harry decorated this table at Tredegar House, Newport. He followed an illustration in an 1874 issue of the* Gardener's Magazine.

48 *Asparagus on toast with a tureen of melted butter.*

49 *Moulding an ox tongue by pressing it against the wall and arching it across a rolling pin. The tongue was then left overnight to set into this position.*

50 *Next day it was glazed and garnished.*

48

49

50

Soyer's gas stove

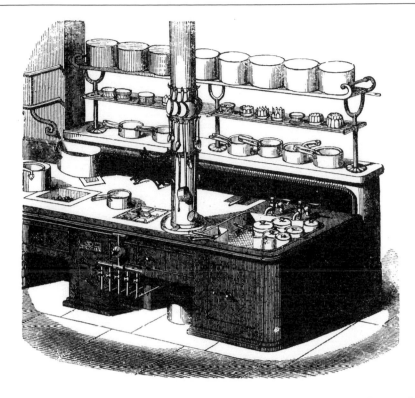

He had it pulled back and enjoyed the screams of surprise from those who had been standing unaware, less than two feet from the fire.

Soyer was probably one of the first chefs to cook on gas. He had two gas stoves of his own design installed into the new kitchen. By virtue of an octagonal-shaped trivet, also his design, and which was neater in shape than the old triangular sort, he was able to have nine stewpans either simmering or boiling on the same stove.

The visitor who had likened the spaciousness of the kitchen to a ballroom and its whiteness to a bride was also taken with another factor. She described it thus:

All-powerful steam, the noise of which salutes your ear as you enter, here performs a variety of offices; it diffuses a uniform heat to large rows of dishes, warms the metal plates, upon which are disposed the dishes that have been called for, and that are in waiting to be sent above; it turns the spits, draws the water, carries up coal, and moves the plate like an intelligent and indefatigable servant.

The originator of all this power, the steam boiler, resided in the scullery. Also in the scullery – in the sink to be exact – was what Soyer called one of the most simple and useful fixtures of a kitchen. Like most buildings in Victorian times, the Reform Club suffered from blocked drains – until, that is, Soyer invented his sink trap bell. This was a copper bell pierced

51 Mushrooms growing on a ridge in the dark interior of the Forcing House at the garden.

with holes like a colander. The sink plug was attached to a rod. Once the bell was screwed over the plug hole, the plug inside could be lowered and raised by pulling a chain attached to the top of the rod. Sink trap bells were eventually fitted all over the club and the design copied and used in other big houses.

Soyer's kitchen with all its refinements was so impressive that a lithograph was made of the whole complex. The walls of the various kitchens, sculleries and larders are waist-high to the scurrying kitchen staff. This allows people looking at the print to see into each room. In the centre is Soyer himself, talking to visitors and gesturing towards his twelve-sided table. Fourteen hundred copies of the print were sold.

A plan of the kitchen was also included in *The Gastronomic Regenerator* written by Soyer and published in 1846. The book is as extraordinary as its title. In addition to a detailed description of the Reform Club's kitchens, which Soyer hopes will benefit readers, he also includes plans for a 'Kitchen of the Wealthy', 'The Bachelor Kitchen', 'The Cottage Kitchen' and 'My Kitchen at Home'. He adds an appropriate list of utensils for each. The book also contains 2000 recipes and, amongst other items, introduces readers to his inventions. There is a detailed description (taken from an earlier book) of his Pagodatique entrée dish. This was inspired by the Chinese custom of serving sauces in little dip-in dishes. The Pagodatique entrée dish has four small dishes fixed around it. This gives anyone using it the choice of having the entrée *au naturel* or of adding any of four different sauces. Four entrées could have a choice of sixteen sauces. Other inventions are an instrument for jointing large birds, thus making

Sink trap bell

them easier to carve; a new method of carving, and an entirely new joint of meat. This joint Soyer invented in April 1846. He called it 'Soyer's Saddle Back of Mutton'. It was two loins and two necks of a sheep trimmed into the form of a double saddle without, as he said, 'interfering in the least with the leg and shoulders, which would cause a serious loss to the butcher'. *The Gastronomic Regenerator* also contains Soyer's designs for attelettes and jelly moulds and the bill of fare for what he called the most 'recherché dinner I ever dressed'. He even bothers to give the names of the tradesmen who supplied goods for this dinner, not to give them a free advertisement but to demonstrate 'the trouble a real gourmet will take to furnish his table'. Such trouble included having a salmon brought to his kitchen direct from the River Severn in Gloucester. It arrived at 7 o'clock and he boiled it ten minutes before the dinner was laid on the table. It is hardly surprising that a book containing such a wealth of information should have inspired the following tribute, written on 24 November 1846, by a club member called Thomas Hall:

Soyer regenerator ... who would be without such a book. It enhances the value of the chef de cuisine of The Reform Club and has introduced quite a *reform* in the Arts of Cookery. Poor Ude is dead, Careme also, Soyer lives, need I say more.

Soyer does still 'live' in a way at the Reform Club, for on special occasions Alan Riddle recreates some of his more exotic dishes. There's 'Dindoneau à la Nelson', which is a turkey dressed to look like a ship in sail, and there's, 'La Crème d'Egypte, à l'Ibrahim Pacha', the dish which was the pièce de résistance of the banquet that Soyer prepared in 1846 for His Highness Ibrahim Pacha. 'La Crème d'Egypte' is a pyramid about $2\frac{1}{2}$ feet high, made of light meringue cake in imitation of solid stones, surrounded by grapes and other fruit. Soyer gave this dish a clever diplomatic touch, for when the pyramid was put before him the Pacha saw on top of it a drawing of his father. He was delighted and lifted the likeness off. Beneath was another surprise, a framed portrait of the Pacha himself!

Soyer's more exotic dishes take time and labour. Alan has discovered that it takes a week to eighteen days to prepare some of them and a whole eight hours to carry a Soyer-type bill of fare up from the kitchen to the banquet room. There is, however, one Soyer creation which is completely the reverse when it comes to time. It is so quick to prepare and so popular that it hasn't been off the club's menu since 1846 – 'Soyer's Lamb Cutlets Reform'. The secret lies in the way the cutlets are trimmed, getting off most of the fat and most of the sinew. Once trimmed they are put into breadcrumbs and cooked within three or four minutes of ordering. They are garnished with julienne of ham, tongue, white of egg, beetroot, gherkin and truffle with Soyer's

The popular lithograph showing 'The Kitchen Department of the Reform Club', 1842

Dindoneau à la Nelson

Reform Sauce poured over the top. The sauce is a slightly toned-down version of the original, because Alan says that people today would find that very spicy and strong on chilli and tarragon.

Alexis Soyer left the Reform Club in 1850. He was certainly missed. Researches into the club's archives reveal a bill which went whizzing down the kitchen's wooden communication tube soon after his departure. It was from the diner at table number 67 and was tersely backed, 'The mutton today was nasty, white, young stuff, tough and uneatable.'

It would take a further chapter to record Soyer's exploits between his leaving the Reform Club and his death nine years later, aged 49: the success of his ultra-portable 'magic' stove and his famous sauces; the way he revolutionised the British Army kitchens at the Crimea and the stove he invented which was used by the army up until the last war. These rank among his major achievements but his small ones, like his invention of an Improved Baking Dish, a Baking Stewing Pan and a Vegetable Drainer, were important enough for Mary Jewry to include in her popular *Every-Day Cookery* published in 1875. Introducing them she says:

It would be unjust to the memory of a great cook if we omitted from our list the culinary utensils invented by the late M. Soyer...

It would have been equally unjust to have omitted Alexis Soyer from a book about the Victorian kitchen.

Victorian Recipes

It's impossible to leave the Victorian kitchen without giving at least a few recipes from that period. The growth in popular education and the general emphasis on self-improvement during Queen Victoria's reign led to the publication of a multitude of recipe books aimed at all classes of society. Some of these recipes were incredibly vague by our standards. It wasn't until Eliza Acton's *Modern Cookery* (published in 1845) and Mrs Beeton's *Book of Household Management* (published in 1861) that exact ingredients and cookery times were clearly set out.

The recipes given here are inevitably just a tiny fraction of those available, but they are representative of the sort of everyday fare that would have been served in houses large and small. The original wording has been left as far as possible to keep the feel of the period, but the recipes themselves have been specially adapted by Ruth Mott so that they can be easily followed and cooked by modern methods. Conversion tables are given below. These are approximate conversions and have been rounded up or down. Never mix metric and imperial measures. Use one system or the other.

WEIGHTS		13	375	MEASUREMENTS	
½oz	10 g	14	400	¼ inch	0.5 cm
1	25	15	425	½	1
2	50	1 lb	450	1	2.5
3	75			2	5
4	110	VOLUME		3	7.5
5	150	1 fl oz	25 ml	4	10
6	175	2	50	5	13
7	200	3	75	6	15
8	225	5 (¼ pint)	150	7	18
9	250	10 (½)	300	8	20.5
10	275	15 (¾)	400	9	23
11	300	1 pint	570	10	25
12	350				

SPRING FRUIT SOUP

Peel and well wash the rhubarb. Blanch it in water for 3 or 4 minutes. Drain and put into a stewpan with the onion, carrot, ham and butter.

Let it stew gently over a slow fire until tender, then add the consommé and breadcrumbs. Boil for about 15 minutes. Skim off all the fat and season with salt and cayenne pepper.

Pass through a tamis and serve with croûtons.

Adapted from *The Cook's Oracle*, Dr William Kitchiner, 1840.

Ruth's note Tinned consommé works well in this recipe if you don't have time to make your own. Blending the soup in a modern food processor or blender is another way of making this soup much more quickly than would have been possible in Victorian days and it's certainly a lot less tiring than tammying!

12 sticks rhubarb
1 medium onion, sliced
1 medium carrot, sliced
½ oz lean ham or bacon, diced
2 oz butter
1¼ pints consommé
1 oz breadcrumbs
salt
cayenne pepper

SERVES 4

JERUSALEM ARTICHOKE SOUP

Put the bacon and vegetables, which should be cut into thin slices, into a stewpan with the butter. Braise these for 15 minutes, keeping them well stirred.

Wash and pare the artichokes and cut them into thin slices. Add them, with ½ pint of stock, to the other ingredients. When these have gently stewed down to a smooth pulp, put in the remainder of the stock. Stir it well, adding the seasoning, and when it has simmered for 5 minutes, pass it through a strainer.

Now pour it back into the stewpan, let it again simmer 5 minutes, taking care to skim it well, and stir into it the boiling milk with 1 tablespoon cream.

Serve with croûtons.

Adapted from Mrs Beeton's *Book of Household Management*, 1861.

Ruth's note Not many people these days want to go to the trouble of making their own white stock and it is much quicker – and easier – to use chicken stock cubes in this recipe. If you do this, however, you should add the seasoning last of all as stock cubes can be quite salty.

1–2 slices lean bacon or ham
¼ head of celery
½ turnip
½ onion
1½ oz butter
2 lb artichokes
2½ pints white stock
salt
cayenne pepper
½ pint milk, boiling
1 tablespoon cream

SERVES 5–6

MULLIGATAWNY SOUP

1 onion, sliced
2 oz butter
2 tomatoes, sliced
2 green chillies, cut fine
curry powder to taste
1 quart good stock
3 eggs

SERVES 4

Fry the onion in the butter, and add the tomatoes, chillies and curry powder. Then pour in the stock and boil for about half an hour. Skim well. Let the soup cool. Beat the whites and yolks of the eggs together, and add to the soup. Stir over the fire until very hot. Serve boiled rice separately.

Adapted from *High-class Cookery Recipes*, Mrs Charles Clarke, 1887.

Ruth's note You must be very careful not to let the soup boil after you've added the eggs, otherwise the eggs will scramble. You can substitute tinned consommé for the home-made stock.

BOILED LEG OF MUTTON

Cut off the shank bone, trim the knuckle, and wash and wipe it very clean. Then put it into a saucepan with enough cold water for it to swim in, and set it over a good fire. As the scum rises, skim it off carefully. Boil the joint for two hours and a half, or according to its weight. When the joint is taken up, put a frill of cut paper round the shank bone. Mash some turnips with a little piece of butter and cream, form them into the shapes of eggs, and garnish the edge of the dish alternately with the turnip balls and with carrots cut into circular forms. Serve with caper sauce in a tureen.

From *Warne's Every-Day Cookery*, edited by Mary Jewry, 1875.

CAPER SAUCE FOR BOILED MUTTON

3 tablespoons capers
1 tablespoon of their liquor
½ pint of melted butter

Chop the capers twice or thrice, and add them with their liquor, to ½ pint of melted butter, made very smoothly. Keep stirring well. Let the sauce just simmer for 2 minutes, and serve in a tureen.

From Mrs Beeton's *Book of Household Management*, 1861.

Ruth's note Boiled leg of mutton was a very popular dish in Victorian days and would have been served both in the servants' hall and to the family of the house.

Pickled nasturtium pods were sometimes used instead of capers in the accompanying sauce – not something I've ever tried myself!

SMALL BEEF STEAK PUDDING

Make into a very firm smooth paste one pound of flour, six ounces of beef suet finely minced, half a teaspoonful of salt, and half a pint of cold water. Use two-thirds of this to line a basin which holds a pint and a half.

Cut a pound of tender steak, free from bone and skin, into pieces and season with salt and pepper well mixed together. Lay it in the crust, pour in a quarter of a pint of water, roll out the cover, close the pudding carefully, tie a floured cloth over, and boil it for three hours and a half.

The water should not come more than half-way up the basin or it will splash over onto the pudding. Check frequently, and add more boiling water as necessary.

Adapted from *Modern Cookery*, Eliza Acton, 1845.

Ruth's note This was popular as a lunch dish for servants. I've often made a version of this for shooting lunches, making a very large pudding using 4lb meat. (Of course, this has to be cooked for much longer than the small version.) It re-heats well and is even better the next day.

For the crust
1 lb plain flour
6 oz beef suet
½ teaspoon salt
½ pint water

For the filling
1 lb rump steak
salt and pepper to taste
¼ pint water

SERVES 2–3

SPRING STEW OF VEAL

Cut two pound of veal, free from fat, into small half-inch thick cutlets; flour them well, and fry them in butter with two small cucumbers sliced, sprinkled with pepper and floured, and twenty-four green gooseberries cut open length-wise and seeded. When the whole is nicely browned, lift it into a thick saucepan, and pour gradually into the pan half a pint, or rather more of boiling water or broth. Add as much salt and pepper as it requires. Give it a minute's simmer, and pour it over the meat, shaking it well round the pan as this is done. Let the veal stew gently from three quarters of an hour to an hour. A bunch of green onions cut small may be added to the other vegetables if liked; and the veal will eat better, if slightly seasoned with salt and pepper before it is floured; a portion of fat can be left on it if preferred.

Adapted from *Modern Cookery*, Eliza Acton, 1845.

Ruth's note I would omit the gooseberries from this recipe and substitute the juice of one lemon which would give the sharpness required.

2 lb veal
2 cucumbers
24 green gooseberries
½ pint water or broth
salt and pepper

SERVES 6

CHICKEN OR FOWL PIE

2 small fowls or 1 large one
a few slices of ham
forcemeat or sausage meat
3 hard-boiled eggs
$\frac{1}{2}$ teaspoon pounded mace
$\frac{1}{2}$ teaspoon grated nutmeg
white pepper and salt to taste
$\frac{1}{2}$ pint water
puff pastry

SERVES 8

Skin and cut up the fowls into joints, and put the neck, legs and backbones in a stew pan with a little water, an onion, a bunch of savory herbs and a blade of mace. Let these stew for about an hour and, when done, strain off the liquor; this is for gravy.

Put a layer of fowl at the bottom of a pie dish, then a layer of ham, then one of forcemeat and hard-boiled eggs cut in rings. Between the layers put a seasoning of pounded mace, nutmeg, pepper and salt. Proceed in this manner until the dish is full, and pour in about half a pint of water. Border the edge of the dish with puff pastry, put on the cover, ornament the top and glaze it by brushing over it the yolk of an egg.

Bake from $1\frac{1}{4}$ to $1\frac{1}{2}$ hours, should the pie be very large, and, when done, pour in at the top the gravy made from the bones.

If to be eaten cold, and wished particularly nice, the joints of the fowls should be boned and placed in the dish with alternate layers of forcemeat; sausage meat may also be substituted for the forcemeat, and is now very much used. When the chickens are boned and mixed with sausage meat, the pie will take about 2 hours to bake. It should be covered with a piece of paper when about half done to prevent the pastry from being dried up or scorched.

Adapted from Mrs Beeton's *Book of Household Management*, 1861.

Ruth's note The oven temperature for this recipe should be gas mark 4, 180°C (350°F). Chicken pies such as this were often served for lunch or at picnics.

STEWED RABBIT AND ONIONS

For this dish an earthenware casserole dish with a close-fitting cover will be required. Cut one rabbit into small pieces, and peel and cut in thin slices two moderate-sized Spanish onions. Fill the casserole dish with alternate layers of rabbit and onion, seasoning well with salt, pepper and mixed herbs between each layer. Put in a few rashers of bacon, and lastly a few more slices of onion. Pour in the stock. Put the cover on the casserole and stew the contents very gently for two hours. When cooked, turn the stew on to a hot dish, and serve.

From *The Encyclopaedia of Practical Cookery*, 1890s.

Ruth's note This makes a lovely lunch dish served with potatoes and a green vegetable.

1 rabbit, jointed
2 medium onions
salt
pepper
mixed herbs
few rashers of bacon
½ pint stock or water

SERVES 4

SAVOURY PUDDING

Soak the bread in the milk until quite soft. Boil the onions in plenty of water; when tender, chop them up very fine. The suet must also be chopped very fine. Mix the bread, onions, suet, oatmeal and sage together. Beat the egg, season to taste, and add to the bread mixture.

   Put the dripping into the pudding tin and make it hot. Pour in the pudding and bake for 45 minutes.

From *Food and Home Cookery*, 1879.

Ruth's note This would have been used in much the same way as we use stuffing today.

3 oz bread
5 fl oz milk
3 large onions
3 oz suet
3 oz oatmeal
1 teaspoon or 6 leaves sage
1 egg
salt and pepper to taste
1 oz dripping

CARDOONS WITH CHEESE

cardoons
red wine
salt
pepper
knob of butter
flour
juice of 1 orange
Parmesan or Cheshire cheese

String the stalks, and cut them in pieces an inch long. Put them into a saucepan with red wine, seasoned with pepper and salt, and stew them till they are tender. Put in a piece of butter rolled in flour and stir until the sauce is of a proper thickness. Put the cardoons into a dish, squeeze the juice of an orange into the sauce, and scrape over them some Parmesan or Cheshire cheese, and then brown them under a grill, but not of too high a colour.

From *The Cottage Gardener and Country Gentleman's Companion*, 30 September, 1856.

Ruth's note Celery may be used instead of cardoons in this recipe.

POTATO SNOW

A favourite way of cooking potatoes.

Choose white, mealy, smooth potatoes. Skin them, boil them carefully, and when they crack pour off the water, and put them to dry on the trivet till quite dry and powdery. Rub them through a coarse wire sieve on the dish they are to go to table on; and do not move it or the flakes will fall and flatten.

From *The Cook and Housewife's Manual*, Mistress Dods, 1837.

Ruth's note I've included this recipe simply to show the extraordinary lengths that Victorian cooks went to in order to present dishes in an unusual way. I used to make a similar dish myself by pushing cooked potatoes through what was known as a 'ricer' – a utensil rather like a huge garlic press. The potato came out in thin strands.

SALMAGUNDI

Turn a deep saucer or a wide teacup upside down on a small dish and arrange round and over it in rows the yolks and whites of hard-boiled eggs, chopped separately, the white meat of roasted veal or fowl, boiled beetroot, nicely seasoned with vinegar and pepper, pickled red cabbage, lean ham, tongue, a few anchovies, and a little parsley, all finely chopped, or anything else that has a good colour and a nice flavour. Make the rows at the bottom wider than the top ones, narrowing them gradually and varying the colours as much as possible and contrasting them nicely; arrange on the top a sprig of curled parsley, and garnish the dish with a border of parsley.

hard-boiled eggs
veal or chicken, cooked
beetroot
pickled red cabbage
lean ham
tongue
anchovies
parsley, chopped

From *The Encyclopaedia of Practical Cookery*, 1890s.

Ruth's note The appeal of this recipe lies in the presentation and you can choose the amounts and ingredients to suit your own requirements. I put a few anchovies across the top in a sort of star-fish pattern which makes a very attractive decoration.

STEWED LETTUCE

Strip off the outer leaves, and cut away the stalks; wash the lettuce with exceeding nicety, and throw into water salted as for all green vegetables. When the leaves are quite tender, which will be in from 20 to 30 minutes, according to their age, lift them out and press the water thoroughly from them. Chop them a little, and heat them in a clean saucepan with a seasoning of pepper and salt, and a small slice of butter. Then dredge in a little flour and stir them well. Add next a small cup of broth, gravy or consommé, boil them quickly until they are tolerably dry, then stir in a little pale vinegar or lemon juice, and serve them as hot as possible.

1 lettuce
pepper
salt
knob of butter
flour
1 cup broth, gravy or
  consommé

From *Modern Cookery*, Eliza Acton, 1845.

Ruth's note Nowadays we tend to use lettuces mostly in salads, but in Victorian days it was quite often cooked. This recipe was a good way of using up surplus lettuce from the kitchen garden and would have been served with roast meat.

GREEN PEAS, TO STEW

2 lb peas
1 lettuce, shredded
1 onion, sliced
butter
pepper
salt

SERVES 6–8

Put into the stew pan 2 lb peas, a lettuce, and an onion sliced, butter, pepper, salt, but no more water than remains about the lettuce after washing. Cook very gently until done.

Adapted from *The Best of Everything*, 1875.

Ruth's note This recipe can be made using frozen peas. Boil them until tender and then add them to the other ingredients. Shake them over the heat until the lettuce wilts.

EGGS WITH ARTICHOKES

6 cooked artichoke bottoms
melted butter
6 poached eggs
cayenne pepper or tarragon
  vinegar

SERVES 6

This should be made with artichoke bottoms but a decidedly nice combination can be made with Jerusalem artichokes. Arrange six cooked artichoke bottoms on a buttered fireproof dish, pour a few drops of melted butter on each, and warm in the oven. Take out the dish, put a nicely trimmed poached egg upon each, sprinkle a dust of cayenne pepper or a drop or two of tarragon vinegar over each, and serve.

When made with Jerusalem artichokes, the purée is the simplest method to choose for the vegetable; line a well buttered fireproof dish with this; dust a fine layer of grated cheese over the surface, dress the poached eggs neatly in hollows scooped out of this bed, and serve.

From *Fifty Breakfasts*, A. K. Herbert, 1894.

Ruth's note The imported French artichokes are best for this recipe – English artichokes tend to be smaller.

This recipe would also make a nice first course for lunch.

SAVOURY EGGS

Chop up a little cold bacon in dice, mix with it chopped parsley and season with pepper and put it in a shallow tart dish. Beat up two eggs with a little salt, a tablespoonful of milk or cream, and pour over the bacon. Bake in a moderate oven until the eggs are set. If liked, a well boiled onion may be mixed with the bacon.

From *Handbook for the Breakfast Table*, Mary Hooper, 1873.

1–2 oz cooked bacon
chopped parsley
pepper
2 eggs
salt
1 tablespoon milk or cream

SERVES 1–2

KEDGEREE

Boil the rice until tender. Boil four eggs very hard and when cold chop them small. Take the remains of any white fish that has been previously boiled, flake it fine and mix all well together, and put the mixture into a stewpan with a lump of fresh butter. Stew it till thoroughly hot, stirring it constantly to prevent its burning. Season it with salt and pepper, and serve it up very hot. Take care not to make it too moist. Cold salmon answers very well for this dish; but haddock, turbot, soles or pike are generally preferred.

From *Warne's Every-Day Cookery*, edited by Mary Jewry, 1875.

Ruth's note I like to make kedgeree using half white and half smoked fish (e.g. smoked haddock – or salmon if you're feeling extravagant!) as it gives a stronger flavour.

4 oz rice
4 eggs
1 lb cooked white fish
butter
salt
pepper

SERVES 4

FINNAN HADDOCK

1 finnan haddock
1–2 tablespoons double cream

SERVES 1

Soak the haddock in cold water for one hour. Take it out, dry it, skin it, and put it into a buttered sauté pan. Pour over it, according to the size of the fish, a tablespoonful or two of cream. Put the pan on the fire, let it come to the boil, and then let it simmer with the lid on till the haddock is cooked. This will probably be in half an hour. Take out the fish, lay it on a hot dish, reduce the sauce till you have to scrape it out of the pan. Put it on the haddock; it gives just a browning look and a nice flavour. Add no seasoning of any kind. Serve the fish very hot.

From *Mrs Roundell's Practical Cookery Book*, 1898.

Ruth's note In the days when I was in service, Finnan haddock was always a popular breakfast dish. There was usually a choice of eggs and bacon, a fish dish and cold meats.

MARROW TOAST

1 marrowbone
toast
salt
pepper
parsley

Get a marrowbone well broken up by the butcher. Take out the marrow in as large pieces as possible, and put them into a stewpan with a little boiling water nicely salted. Let the marrow boil for a minute, then strain it through a fine strainer. Have ready a thin toast, place the marrow on it before the fire and let it remain until cooked, which will be in about 5 minutes. Sprinkle over it a little pepper and salt, and a small teaspoonful of parsley chopped very fine. Serve very hot.

From *Handbook for the Breakfast Table*, Mary Hooper, 1873.

Ruth's note I used to cook a version of this dish in which marrowbones were baked with a flour and water crust over each end to prevent the juices escaping. They were then served in a napkin, one per person, and the diners would extract the marrow from the bone themselves.

Scotch Woodcock

Toast the bread and butter it well on both sides. Take the anchovies, washed, scraped and chopped fine, and put them between the slices of toast. Have ready the yolks of four eggs well beaten, and half a pint of cream, which set over the fire to thicken but not boil. Pour it over the toast and serve it to table as hot as possible.

4 slices bread
butter
10 anchovies
4 egg yolks
½ pint cream

SERVES 4

From *The Cook's Oracle*, Dr W. Kitchiner, 1840.

Ruth's note A tasty and less fiddly alternative is to use Gentlemen's relish or anchovy essence instead of the anchovies.

Hash

'I am well aware that in your homes it is not a common every-day occurrence for you to dress a large joint of meat, from which enough would be left for one or more days' dinner; but still it may, and does some-times occur, that you have cold meat at your disposal, upon which you may exercise your knowledge in domestic economy. Besides, some of you who are living close to noblemen and gentlemen's mansions in the country, or otherwise, may perhaps stand a chance of now and then receiving a donation of this kind. And whenever you have any cold meat, I advise you to cook it up into stews of various kinds described in this work, or else make it into a hash as follows:

2 onions
pepper
salt
1 pint water
cold meat, thinly sliced
a little flour

First, chop two onions fine, and put them to boil with pepper and salt and a pint of water, in a saucepan for ten minutes, then throw in the meat cut in thin slices, mixed with a little flour; boil all together gently for ten minutes longer, and pour the hash into a dish containing either some ready boiled potatoes, or else some slices of toasted bread.'

From *A Plain Cookery Book for the Working Classes*, Charles E. Francatelli, 1861.

Ruth's note This was a very popular supper dish for staff.

BLACKCURRANT CREAM ICE

1 lb blackcurrants
*½ pint syrup, made with 8 oz
sugar and ½ pint water*
½ pint double cream

To decorate

*Crystallised cherries, candied
angelica, preserved fruits.*

SERVES 4

Pick the stalks off the blackcurrants, stir and mash them over the fire for 5 minutes, then pass them through a fine hair sieve. Mix the syrup, at 32 degrees, with the blackcurrant purée and cream.

When well beaten together, turn the mixture into a freezer, and work till stiff. Put the cream in a fluted mould, close it, pack in ice, and leave till frozen.

Dip the mould in lukewarm water, wipe it, and turn the cream out on to a fancy dish. Decorate with crystallised cherries, candied angelica cut into points, and garnish round the dish with preserved apples and pears, or other fruit. Surmount the whole with an ornamental attelette, and set back in the ice-chest to keep cold until wanted.

This is reckoned to be one of the finest flavoured and handsomest sweets that can be prepared.

From *The Encyclopaedia of Practical Cookery*, 1890s.

Ruth's note No one in their right mind would want to use a Victorian ice-pail to make this! Use a modern ice-cream maker, or put the mixture in the freezer, stirring from time to time during the freezing process. The result will be just as good.

BROWN BREAD PUDDING

1 stale brown loaf
3 oz caster sugar
1 lb fresh cherries
½ teaspoon vanilla essence
grated rind of one lemon
5 fl. oz milk
5 fl. oz cream
4 eggs
2 oz sugar
7 fl. oz water

SERVES 4

Put 5 ounces of brown breadcrumbs into a basin with the caster sugar and three-quarters of a pound of cherries, stoned, the vanilla, and grated lemon rind. Boil the milk and pour it over the crumbs and fruit. Whip the cream to a stiff froth and add it to the crumbs. Separate the eggs. Add the yolks of four eggs, one at a time, and the white of two eggs, whisked to a stiff froth, to the mixture.

Pre-heat the oven to gas mark 4, 180°C (350°F).

Butter a pint mould and pour in the mixture. Cover it with buttered paper, and steam or bake one hour and a quarter. Turn it out onto a hot dish, and serve with sauce made with two ounces of sugar, 7 fluid ounces of water, and a quarter of a pound of cherries.

From *High-class Cookery Recipes*, Mrs Charles Clarke, 1887.

OUR QUEEN'S PUDDING – THE ROYAL VICTORIA

Fill a rather deep, dome-shaped cake mould with preserved or tinned peaches; make a large quantity of good calves' feet jelly, rather a little stronger than usual, and colour part of it a pretty pink; pour some of the jelly into the mould, so that it will be at the top about an inch deep. When cold, pour in a little more of the jelly, a pale lemon colour, and when that is set, pour the mould full of the rest of the jelly, coloured amber. When quite firm, turn out in a dish, with a pretty light ornamental border of crystallised rings, kept together with barley sugar; spin it all round with sugar, and over the top, by dipping a fork, and running it round quickly. When the sugar gets too hard, hold the pan over the fire, a minute; frost it all over with pink and white sugar.

preserved or tinned peaches jelly in different colours – pink, lemon, amber

From Mrs Somerville's *Cookery and Domestic Economy*, 1862.

Ruth's note Packet jelly can be used instead of calves' feet jelly but a little more gelatine should be added.

CHRISTMAS PLUM PUDDING

First, put the flour, suet, and all the fruit in a large pan. Mix these well together, and having made a deep hole in the middle thereof with your fist, add the salt, sugar, and allspice, and half a pint of the milk, or beer, to dissolve them. Next, add the four eggs, and the remaining pint of milk or beer. Mix all vigorously together with the hand, tie up the pudding in a well-greased and floured cloth, and boil it for at least four hours, taking care that the water boils before the pudding is put into the pot to boil. When done, turn the pudding out on its dish.

2 lb plain flour
1 lb chopped suet
12 oz raisins
12 oz currants
12 oz apples, peeled and chopped
good pinch salt
12 oz sugar
½ oz ground allspice
1½ pints milk or beer
4 eggs

From *A Plain Cookery Book for the Working Classes*, Charles E. Francatelli, 1861.

Ruth's note You can make this lighter in texture by using half flour and half breadcrumbs.

SERVES 8

TREACLE PUDDING

4 oz currants

4 oz suet

1 breakfast cupful
breadcrumbs

1 breakfast cupful self-
raising flour

1 tablespoon sugar

½ teaspoon salt

1 teaspoon ground ginger

½ teaspoon carbonate of soda

¼ teaspoon cream of tartar

8 oz treacle

1 egg

water

SERVES 4–6

Wash and dry the currants, and chop up the suet very finely. Put into a basin all the dry ingredients (the bread, flour, sugar, currants, suet, salt, ginger, carbonate of soda, and cream of tartar) and mix them well, after which add the treacle, stirring it about.

Beat up the egg and mix with it a teacupful of water; pour this in and mix all well together. It should be quite moist without being at all sloppy.

Put it into a shape or basin well rubbed with dripping or butter, and cover with a buttered paper. Place it in a pot in which there is half an inch of boiling water. Put the lid closely on the pot and steam for two and a half hours, then turn out and serve.

N.B. If more water is required to moisten the pudding properly, it must be added; but it is best not to put more among the egg in case it should not be required.

From *Household Cookery*, Mrs Black, 1896.

Ruth's note This makes a lovely, dark-coloured pudding. Surprisingly it's very light and would make a good alternative to the more traditional Christmas pudding.

FIVE O'CLOCK TEA SCONES

Pre-heat the oven to gas mark 6, 200°C (400°F).

Mix the baking powder and salt into the flour, rub the butter well into the flour, beat up the eggs and add them with the milk. Turn the mixture on to a floured board, and make into a light dough; give it one roll with a rolling-pin very lightly, letting it be about half an inch thick. Cut with a round cutter about the size of a saucer, and marks across each twice with a knife, so that they will break into four pieces when baked.

Bake on floured tins, from 15 to 20 minutes. Directly they are taken from the oven, cut them open, put plenty of butter on, place the pieces together again, and serve hot.

Half this quantity makes a good plateful.

From *The Menu Cookery Book for Moderate People with Moderate Incomes*, Mary Davies, 1885.

Ruth's note In Victorian times scones were often served at breakfast, along with rolls and brioches.

2 teaspoons baking powder
½ teaspoon salt
1 lb flour
6 oz butter
2 eggs
½ pint milk

PLAIN SEED CAKE

Pre-heat the oven to gas mark 4, 180°C (350°F).

Cream the butter and sugar together and fold in the flour and cornflour. Add the caraway seeds.

Separate the eggs. Beat the yolks and mix into the flour. Whisk the whites until fairly stiff and fold into the flour mixture.

Bake in a greased, lined 10-in. cake tin for 1½–2 hours.

Adapted from Mrs Somerville's *Cookery and Domestic Economy*, 1862.

Ruth's note Sprinkle caster sugar on top of the cake before you put it in the oven – this gives it a nice gooey crust.

1 lb butter
1 lb caster sugar
1 lb self-raising flour
2 oz cornflour
1 oz caraway seeds
10 eggs

AN EXCELLENT CAKE THAT WILL KEEP GOOD A YEAR

12 oz butter
12 oz brown sugar
12 oz self-raising flour
12 oz currants
12 oz raisins
1 oz almonds
1 oz lemon peel
1 oz orange peel
5 eggs
1 wineglass brandy

Pre-heat the oven to gas mark 4, 180°C (350°F).

Cream the butter and sugar together and fold in the flour. Mix in the other dry ingredients.

Beat the eggs and add to the mixture. Finally add the brandy.

Bake in a greased, lined 8–9 in. cake tin for 1 hour. Reduce the oven temperature to gas mark 2, 150°C (300°F) and bake for a further hour or until cooked.

From *The Cottage Gardener*, 29 August, 1850.

Ruth's note Fruit cakes tend to improve with keeping. The raisins and currants tend to dry out during cooking, but if the cake is left they absorb moisture and plump up again.

QUINCE FOR THE TEA TABLE

Bake ripe quinces thoroughly; when cold, strip off the skins, place them in a glass dish and sprinkle with white sugar, and serve them with cream. They make a fine-looking dish for the tea table, and a more luscious and inexpensive one than the same fruit made into sweetmeats. Those who once taste the fruit thus prepared will probably desire to store away a few bushels in the fall to use in the above manner.

From *The Complete Every-Day Cookery Book*, 1866.

Ruth's note This would make a lovely dessert for a light lunch.

RED CURRANT MARMALADE

Squeeze some ripe red currants through a coarse muslin; to every pint of juice put a pound of preserving sugar; boil it very well; when nearly boiled to a jelly, have some bunches of large white currants nicely picked, throw them in, and boil five minutes; it should turn out stiff and transparent.

red currants
preserving sugar

To decorate
white currants

From *The Best of Everything*, 1875.

Ruth's note The white currants are left in the marmalade for decoration. Boiling them before putting them in the marmalade prevents them from fermenting.

PLUM OR DAMSON CHEESE

Put a quantity of plums into a jar, and stand the jar in a saucepan of water on the fire; when quite soft pulp them through a sieve, and to every pound of pulp, add one pound of preserving sugar, and one ounce of sweet almonds, blanched and pounded, with four bitter almonds; boil all together till the fruit will form a stiff jelly. If the plums are very juicy, some of the juice may be taken off the fruit.

plums
preserving sugar
sweet almonds

From *The Best of Everything*, 1875.

CHILLI OR CAYENNE WINE

50 fresh red chillies or ¼ oz cayenne pepper
½ pint brandy, white wine or claret

MAKES ½ PINT

Pound and steep 50 fresh red chillies or a quarter of an ounce of cayenne pepper in half a pint of brandy, white wine, or claret for fourteen days. This, which takes up a larger proportion of the flavour of cayenne than of its fire, will be found a very warm auxiliary to season and finish soups and sauces.

From *The Cottage Gardener and Country Gentleman's Companion*, 30 September, 1856.

Ruth's note This sounds very like the tabasco sauce of today (minus the brandy!).

BARLEY WATER

2 oz pearl barley
1 pint cold water
2 quarts boiling water
sugar to taste

MAKES 1 QUART

Wash the barley in cold water. Put it into a saucepan with the above proportion of cold water, and when it has boiled for about ¼ hour, strain off the water and add the 2 quarts of fresh boiling water. Boil it until the liquid is reduced one half; strain into a jug to cool, add the sugar and it will be ready for use.

It may be flavoured with lemon peel after being sweetened, or a small piece may be simmered with the barley. When the invalid may take it, a little lemon juice gives this pleasant drink in illness a very nice flavour.

Adapted from Mrs Beeton's *Book of Household Management*, 1861.

Ruth's note This recipe makes a lovely, smooth drink. I used to make it every day for use in the nursery or sick room.

SHERBET OF WATER MELON

Let the melon be cut in half, and the inside of the fruit be worked up and mashed with a spoon, till it assumes the consistency of a thick pulp. Introduce into this as much pounded white candy or sugar as may suit your taste, a wine glassful of fresh rose-water, and two wine glasses of sherry. Pour, when strained, the contents into a jug, and fill your tumblers when needed.

From *The Complete Every-Day Cookery Book*, 1866.

Ruth's note This makes a very agreeable drink in summer.

1 water melon
sugar to taste
1 wine glass rose-water
2 wine glasses sherry

CLARET CUP

Into a quart vessel put the sherry, nutmeg, cloves, sugar, the juice and rind of one-third of a lemon, and either six small leaves of mint, two slices of cucumber or a sprig of borage. To these ingredients add a little claret, and having well stirred the mixture allow it to stand for twenty minutes. Then with a spoon remove the cloves, lemon peel, cucumber etc. When the cup is required for use, pour in two bottles of soda water and fill up with claret.

From Octavius Morgan's papers.

2 glasses dry sherry
$\frac{1}{6}$ nutmeg, grated
8 cloves
2 tablespoons sugar
juice and rind of $\frac{1}{3}$ lemon
6 small leaves mint, or 2 slices cucumber, or a sprig of borage
claret

SHERRY COBBLER

Put the ingredients into a tumbler and fill the tumbler up with planed or crushed ice. A fresh ripe strawberry or raspberry or two, or a slice of fresh pineapple, is a real improvement.

From *The Best of Everything*, 1875.

$1\frac{1}{2}$ glasses sherry
$\frac{1}{2}$ glass Curaçao
1 teaspoon raspberry syrup
thin slices orange peel
1 teaspoon sugar

BIBLIOGRAPHY

·

Acton, E., *Modern Cookery*, Longman, Brown, Green & Longmans, 1845 and 1855.
Mrs Beeton's *Book of Household Management*, S. O. Beeton, 1861.
Mrs Beeton's *Cookery Book and Household Guide*, Ward Lock, Bowden & Co., 1893.
The Best of Everything, Frederick Warne & Co., 1875.
Black, Mrs, *Household Cookery and Laundry Work*, William Collins Sons & Co. Ltd, 1882.
Buckton, C. M. *Food & Home Cookery*, Longmans, Green & Co., 1879.
The Canned Food Reference Manual, American Can Company, 1943.
Cobbett, A. *The English Housekeeper & Manual of Domestic Management*,
A. A. Cobbett, 1851.
Dallas, E. S. *Kettner's Book of the Table*, Dulau & Co., 1877.
Delamere, Dr and Mrs, *Wholesome Fare – a Sanitary Cook-Book*, Crosby, Lockwood &
Co., 1878.
De Salis, Mrs, *Entrées à la Mode*, Longmans, Green & Co., 1900.
Dictionary of Cookery, Cassell, Petter, Galpin & Co., 1876.
The Enquirer's Oracle, Ward Lock & Co., 1884.
Faunthorpe, Rev. J. P. (ed.), *Household Science*, Edward Stanford, 1881.
Francatelli, C. E. *The Cook's Guide and Housekeeper's & Butler's Assistant*,
Richard Bentley, 1868.
Francatelli, C. E. *A Plain Cookery Book for the Working Classes*, Routledge, Warne &
Routledge, 1861.
Garrett, T. F. (ed.) *The Encyclopaedia of Practical Cookery*, L. Upcott Gill, 1890.
Gill, J. Thompson, *The Complete Confectioner*, M. A. Donohue & Co., 1890.
Gore, Mrs, *Sketches of English Character*, Richard Bentley, 1846.
Herbert, A. K. *Fifty Breakfasts*, Edward Arnold, 1894.
Hooper, M. *Handbook for the Breakfast Table*, Griffith and Farran, 1873.
The Housewife's Reason Why, Houlston & Sons, 1869.
Jewry, M. (ed.), *Warne's Every-Day Cookery*, Frederick Warne & Co., 1875.
Kerr, R. *The Gentleman's House or How to Plan English Residences*, John Murray, 1864.
Kitchiner, Dr W. *The Cook's Oracle*, Robert Cadell, Edinburgh, 1840.
Manners and Tone of Good Society by A Member of the Aristocracy (Second edition), Frederick
Warne & Co., 1879.
Marshall, Mrs A. B. *Cookery Book*, Simpkin, Marshall, Hamilton, Kent & Co., 1890.
Newsholme, A. *Domestic Economy*, Swan, Sonnenschein & Co., 1897.
Panton, J. E. *From Kitchen to Garret*, Ward & Downey, 1888.
The Servants' Practical Guide, Frederick Warne & Co., 1880.
Soyer, A. *Délassements Culinaires*, 1845.
Soyer, A. *The Gastronomic Regenerator*, Simpkin, Marshall & Co., 1846.
Taylor, E. H. *The Story of Preserved Foods*, Angus Watson & Co. Ltd, 1922.
Thompson, Sir Henry, *Food and Feeding*, Frederick Warne & Co., 1891.
Tinned Foods and How to Use Them, Ward Lock, Bowden & Co. Ltd., 1893.
Walsh, J. H. *A Manual of Domestic Economy*, Routledge, 1857 and 1890.
Williams, W. Mattieu, *The Chemistry of Cookery*, Chatto & Windus, 1885.
Young, H. M. *Domestic Cookery: with special reference to Cooking by Gas*,
H. M. Young, 1886.

INDEX

·

Acton, Eliza, 23, 84, 87,
    93, 97, 154, 165
aerated water, 155
air-baths, 115
Aldenham, Lord, 81
American ovens, 61
Anti-Adulteration
    Association, 107
Appert, Nicholas, 110
apples, 113
apricots, 98–9
Army & Navy Co-
    operative, 106–7
Arnison, Alison, 10, 13,
    36, 71–2, 74–5, 84, 101,
    126, 142
artichokes, 89–90
asparagus, 83, 84–5, 113
'At Homes', 133–5, 136
Athenaeum Club, 82
attelettes, 150
Australian Meat Agency,
    158

bacon, 102, 119
bain-marie, 61, 117
balls, 152
'bamboo', 100
bananas, 113
Barker, John, 88
barley water, 154
Barry, Charles, 159
beans, 100–1
Beckett, Edwin, 81
beef tea, 156
beer, 41, 153
Beeton, Isabella, 23, 100,
    117, 120, 127–9, 158,
    165
The Best of Everything, 85,
    87, 94
beverages, 153–6
birds:
    at dinner, 144–5
    plucking, 36
birthday cakes, 137
biscuits, 138
Black, Mrs, 56, 156

black lead, 55–6
blackcurrants, 95–6
bomb moulds, 66–7
Bonning, May, 62
bottle jacks, 52
bottling, 97–9
boyfriends, 44
braising pans, 60
bread, 37, 115–17, 157
breakfast, 41, 115–24
Brillat-Savarin, Anthelme,
    143, 145
broad beans, 82
broccoli, 87
Brummell, Beau, 81
Brunel, Isambard
    Kingdom, 129
Brussels sprouts, 86
Buckton, Catherine M., 75
budgeting, 79
Burton, William S., 62–3
butlers, 16, 18, 33, 37, 45,
    46, 144
butler's pantry, 18
butter, 102, 109–10

cabbage, 86
cakes, 57, 127, 136
Calais sand, 70, 72, 73
candles, 18, 56
canned foods, 110–14
cardoon, 92
Carême, Marie Antoine,
    28
carpets, cleaning, 76
carrots, 82
catsup, 99–100
cauliflower, 87
champagne, 154
Chapman, Mr, 101
charcoal stoves, 60, 93
charity, 157–8
chefs, 27–8, 38, 120, 152
cherries, 99
chicken gas, 58
chickens, 118, 144
children, 126–7, 136–7,
    157–8

china:
    closets, 16
    washing up, 71–2
Chinese artichokes, 90
Chirk Castle, 57, 74, 148–
    9
chopping blocks, 13
church, 46
Church of England
    Temperance Society,
    156
cleanliness, 69–77
clothes, scullery maids', 34
coal, 57
Cobbett, Anne, 30, 69
Cochin China chickens,
    118
cocoa, 122, 155, 156
coffee, 122, 129–30, 156
Cole, Sir Henry, 24
colewort, 86–7
collard, 86–7
Condy's fluid, 71
consommé, 141–2
cook-generals, 32
cookery books, 23, 58, 141
cookery lessons, 23–5
cooks, 20, 23, 28–33, 45,
    83
co-operative stores, 105
Copley, Esther, 62
copper pots, 63, 73–5
coppers, boiling, 14
corned beef, 114
cornflour, 109, 147
The Cottage Gardener, 96
Crosby, Mrs, 28, 36, 45,
    74, 132
Crosse and Blackwell, 112
cucumber, 135
Cudlip, Mrs Pender, 23
cupboards, 13
'cups', 154

dairies, 15–16
D'Albignac, 147–8
Dallas, E. S., 60, 100
Davis, Joseph, 56

De Salis, Harriet A., 141
Delamere, Dr, 48, 141
Delamere, Mrs, 48
Denyer, Mr, 98
desserts, 139, 146
digesters, 77–8
dinner, 29–30, 38, 41, 139–46
disinfectant, 71
Dodson, Harry, 7, 8, 81, 82–3, 84–5, 89–90, 95–7, 99, 120, 129
doors, 14
drains, 71, 161–2
dressers, 13
drinks, 153–6
dripping, 32, 60, 78–9
Dubois, Urbain, 150
duckboards, 13
Durand, Peter, 110
dustbins, 71
Dutch ovens, 117

eels, 38
egg boilers, 68
eggs, 102, 103, 109, 117–19, 156
Elizabeth, Queen Mother, 32
Ellice, Edward, 159
Emmit, Mrs, 148
enamelled pots, 63
entrées, 113–14, 143, 160, 162
equipment, 12–13, 51–68

fat, 78–9
Faunthorpe, Reverend, 79
First World War, 23
fish, 110–11, 120–1, 125, 148–9, 160
fish kettles, 143
fish larders, 15
floors, 13, 69–70
flour chests, 13
flues, sweeping, 54–5
followers (boyfriends), 44
food:
  canned, 110–14
  fruit and vegetables, 81–92
  keeping hot, 12–13
  preserving, 93–102
  shopping for, 103–14

footmen, 46
Fortnum and Mason, 93
Fox, Gladys, 13
Francatelli, Charles Elme, 28, 158
Franklin, Dr, 115
French beans, 83–4, 101
French ovens, 117
fruit, 83, 103
  bottling, 97–9
  for breakfast, 122
  desserts, 139, 146
  jam-making, 94, 95–7
  puddings, 127
  tinned, 113
  wines, 155

gadgets, 68
galantines, 125–6
game, 36, 102, 144–5
gardeners, 81, 83, 103
The Gardener's Chronicle, 109
garlic, 91
garnishes, 149–52
Garrett, Theodore, 88
gas stoves, 57–8, 93, 161
gelatine, 77, 109, 145–6
Gladstone, W. E., 93
glasses, washing up, 72
glaze, 78
globe artichokes, 90
glycerine, 75
gooseberries, 94, 96, 98, 113, 154
grapes, 99
greengages, 98–9
gridirons, 61
grilling, 61
groceries, 103–14

Hall, Thomas, 163
ham, curing, 101–2
hampers, 103, 107
hand care, 75
Hardy, Mrs, 74, 149
hasteners, 52
head gardeners, 81, 83, 103
Herbert, A. Kenney ('Wyvern'), 117, 121
Hibberd, Shirley, 86–7
holidays, 49
Holmes, Lucy, 137
Hooper, Mary, 115, 119, 155

horseradish, 128–9
hotels, 38, 111
housekeepers, 16–18, 45
Housekeeper's Guide, 73
housemaids, 28
Howard de Walden, Lord and Lady, 57
hunt breakfasts, 124
Huntley and Palmer, 106
hygiene, 69–77

ice, 64–6, 160
ice caves, 67
ice chests, 65
ice cream, 65–8, 133
ice houses, 64, 102
ice pits, 64
invalids, 156
iron, in diet, 126

jam jars, 97
jam-making, 93–7
jellies, 109, 145–6
Jennings, Mr, 97
Jerusalem artichokes, 89–90
Jewry, Mary, 164
The Journal of Horticulture, 82

Kerr, Joan, 136
Kerr, Robert, 18
ketchup, 100
kettles, 73
Kettner's Book of the Table, 60, 91, 100, 145
kidney beans, 84
Kingsley, Charles, 155
kippers, 121
kitcheners, 52, 54
kitchenmaids, 20, 25, 32, 37–40, 45, 46
kitchens:
  equipment, 51–68
  hygiene, 69–77
  lay-out, 11–18
  ranges, 51–60
Kitchiner, Dr William, 23, 30, 39, 82, 142
knives, 72–3
koumiss, 156

Labaube, Mr, 149
lady's maids, 20–3, 46

larders, 14–15
larding, 144
Lavers, Mrs Gwen, 41
Leeds School Board, 24
lemonade, 154
Liebig, Justus von, 107–9
Line, Arthur, 68
linoleum, 70
liqueurs, 155
lobster, 110, 148
Louis the Magnificent, 64
lucifer matches, 56
luncheon, 41, 125–32

maids, 16
  housemaids, 28
  kitchenmaids, 20, 25,
    32, 37–40, 45, 46
  lady's maids, 20–3, 46
  maids-of-all-work, 42,
    77
  parlourmaids, 46
  scullery maids, 34–7,
    40
Malleville, Viscountess
  de, 159
Manual of Domestic
  Economy, 30, 78, 111,
  138
margarine, 110
Marshall, Mrs A. B., 24–5,
  89, 143, 145
Martin, David, 94
Martineaus, 94
matches, 56
meat:
  breakfast dishes, 121
  at dinner, 144
  larders, 14–15
  at luncheon, 125–6
  preserving, 101–2
  roasting, 51–4, 144–5
  tinned, 111–12, 114
Mège-Mouriès, 110
menus, 38, 48, 49, 146
milk, 103, 113, 153
mint julep, 154
mistress of the house, 19–
  26
Moore Ede, Rev. W.,
  158
Morello cherries, 99
Morgan, Octavius, 81–2,
  101
Mott, Ruth, 9 et passim

moulds:
  ice cream, 66–7
  jelly, 145
mulled egg, 156
mushroom ketchup, 100
mushrooms, 120

Napoleon I, Emperor, 110
Napoleon III, Emperor,
  110
nasturtium seeds, 100
nectarines, 155
Northwich, 101
nursery tea, 136–8

oil cloth, 70
omelettes, 119
onions, 91, 99
ovens:
  American ovens, 61
  Dutch ovens, 117
  French ovens, 117
  gas stoves, 57–8
  ranges, 56–7
  roasters, 52–4
ox tongue, 149
oysters, 110–11

packaging, groceries, 107–
  9
Panton, Jane Ellen, 44–5,
  63, 71, 105, 153
pantries, 14
Parkesine, 70
parlourmaids, 46
pastry rooms, 16
peaches, 98–9, 155
pears, 113
peas, 81–2, 100, 112
Peek Frean, 106
Penny Dinner Movement,
  158
percentage system, 33
perks, cook's, 32–3
pestles and mortars, 13
pets, 25–6
Pettit, Margaret, 70
pheasant shoots, 131–2
pickling, 99–101, 113
picnics, 127–9, 154
pies, 147
pigeon pie, 147
pin-rails, 13
pineapples, 113, 114, 146
Pink, Edward, 93

plate racks, 14, 72
plums, 97–8
Polson, John, 109
porridge, 122
potatoes, 88–9, 132, 157
pots and pans, 63, 73–4
poultry, 118, 144
'Poultry Mania', 118
prayers, 45–6, 123
preserving, 93–102
puddings, 127

quenelles, 113–14

railways, 49, 129
ranges, 51–60
raspberries, 96–7, 99
recipe books, 23, 30–2
redcurrants, 96
Reform Club, 158, 159–64
refrigerators, 65
religion, 45–6, 123
Riddle, Alan, 159, 163–4
roasting meat, 51–4,
  144–5
Robinson, Thomas, 51
Romford, Count, 52–4
Royal Institution, 52
Rundell, Mrs, 23
runner beans, 101

safes, 18
salad dressings, 147–8
salads, 144, 147
Salisbury, Marquis of, 149
salmon, 110, 148–9, 163
salsify, 92
salting, 100–1
sandwiches, 129, 135, 147
saucepans, 63, 73
sausages, 119
savings banks, 43–4
savouries, 146
sawdust, 70
scales, 64
schools, cookery lessons,
  23–5
scones, 115–16
scorzonera, 92
screens, 62, 160–1
scrubbing, 69–70
sculleries, 14, 161–2
scullery maids, 34–7, 40
seed cake, 136

servants:
  chefs, 27–8, 38, 120, 152
  cooks, 20, 23, 28–33, 45,
    83
  demand for, 19–20
  housemaids, 28
  kitchenmaids, 20, 25,
    32, 37–9, 45, 46
  lady's maids, 20–3, 46
  maids, 16
  maids-of-all-work, 77
  meals, 39–42
  parlourmaids, 46
  scullery maids, 34–7, 40
  servants' halls, 40
  social life, 48–50
  time off, 46–9
  wages, 33–4, 37, 39,
    42–4
The Servants' Practical
  Guide, 28, 39, 41, 123
serving dishes, 12–13
serving hatches, 12
serving rooms, 12
Sharp, James, 57
shelves, 13
shooting luncheons,
  131–2
shopping, 103–14
Shrewsbury's Portable
  Gas Oven, 57
sieves, 63–4, 73
silver, cleaning, 75–6
sinks, 14
skewers, 150
Skuse, E., 97
smells, 11–12, 71
smoke jacks, 51
smoking, 101–2
snow stacks, 64
'Snowfire', 75
soap, 18, 36, 70
sorbets, 144
soufflés, 12, 67
soups, 141–3, 157, 158

Soyer, Alexis, 89, 129–30,
  158, 159–64
spinach, 85–6
spits, 51
sponge cakes, 136–7
spun sugar, 150–1
stairs, 14
Stanley's Patent Heat
  Conductors, 68, 136
stewing pans, 60, 93
still rooms, 16, 93
stockpots, 78, 141
store rooms, 14, 17–18
stoves:
  gas, 57–8, 93, 161
  ranges, 51–60
strainers, 63–4
strawberries, 99
sugar, 93–5
  spun, 150–1
supper, 42, 147–52
sweets, 145–6

Table Jellies Association,
  145
tables, scrubbing, 69–70
tammying, 142–3
Tate & Lyle, 94
tea (drink), 122, 133–5,
  153, 156
tea (meal), 42, 133–8
tea leaves, 76
Thackeray, William
  Makepeace, 153
thermometers, 56
Thompson, Sir Henry,
  135
Thompson Bros, 101
tiles, 13
tinned foods, 110–14
toast, 121–2
toast water, 155–6
tomatoes, 148
tongue, 149
tradesmen, 33

truck shops, 105
turbot, 143

Ude, Louis Eustache, 23

Vatel, 64
vegetables:
  cooking, 36
  at dinner, 145
  kitchen gardens, 81–92,
    103
  pickling, 99–101
  preparation, 36
  stores, 15
  tinned, 112–13
Victoria, Queen, 28, 90,
  118, 129, 158
Victoria plums, 97–8
Victoria Sandwich, 136
vine leaves, 99
vinegar, 97, 99

wages, 33–4, 37, 39, 42–4,
  157
Walsh, J. H., 30, 111, 138
washing, 71
washing up, 71–2
waste, 77–9
water, drinking, 153, 155
Webster, Augusta, 79–80
wedding breakfasts, 123
weighing food, 64
whisks, 68
Williams, W. Mattieu,
  112, 133–5
windows, 13
wine, 154–5
wine cellars, 18
Woodward, Colonel, 82
Woolley, Pat, 34–6
The World, 25
Wright, Hilda, 148–9
'Wyvern' (A. Kenney
  Herbert), 117, 121

Young, Miss H. M., 58

PICTURE CREDITS

•